Introduction   Ezra, Nehemiah and Esther are the last three books classi-
fied under the historical section of the Old Testament.
Chronologically the group is correctly located in our Bibles, because here are recorded the last events of Old Testament history (i.e., up to about 415 B.C.).* But the historical setting of these books is often obscured in the mind
of the Bible reader because the books that follow them
(poetical and prophetical books through Zephaniah) in our
present Bible arrangement actually revert back in time.
Chart A may help to show the real setting of these last
three historical books (Ezra, Nehemiah, Esther)

LOCATION OF EZRA-NEHEMIAH-ESTHER IN THE OLD TESTAMENT CANON

Chart A

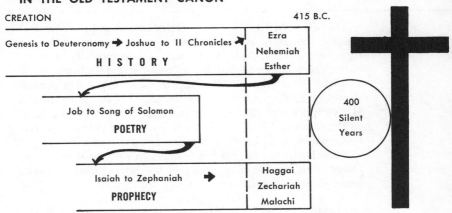

* Actually, the narrative of the book of Esther is dated between chapters
6 and 7 of Ezra.

1

Observe on the diagram the notation "400 silent years." This period up to the time of Christ is so called because the Bible records no history of this period, and no book of the Bible was written during this time.

The best preparation for the study of Ezra, Nehemiah and Esther is a study of the books just before them: Kings and Chronicles. In these books are recorded the ups and downs (mostly downs!) of the two kingdoms of God's chosen people—Israel and Judah—and of their eventual fall and captivity in foreign lands as a divine judgment for sin. The overall account is a classic illustration of the eternal law of returns, a law of cause and effect. The effect was judgment; the cause was sin.

When we come to Ezra and Nehemiah,† we are in a new and bright era of Israel's history—the period of *restoration*, involving a return from captivity to the homeland of Canaan. Fix in your mind the following simple outline of the context of Ezra and Nehemiah as you begin your study in this manual:

Kings and Chronicles		Ezra, Nehemiah
CAUSE →	EFFECT →	SEQUEL
SIN →	JUDGMENT →	RESTORATION
(during the kingdom years)	(captivity)	(return to the land)

There would have been no restoration for Israel were it not for the grace of God. The restoration was surely not deserved. And, before there was even a captivity, the restoration was scheduled on a prophetic timetable by a gracious God who, in the forthcoming captivity period, would be calling out of the communities of Jewish exiles in Babylon a remnant of believers whom He could bring back to the promised land. With these He would perpetuate His covenanted blessings for the generations to come.

Such is the evangel of the books you are about to study. Other great truths shine forth in the books; that of God's grace shines the brightest.

*   *   *

† Esther is intentionally omitted in this reference. As will be seen later, the book of Esther records events of the same general period as Ezra and Nehemiah, but its theme is not one of *restoration*.

The following suggestions are given especially for study groups, such as a home Bible class. If you are studying alone, most of the suggestions will also apply to you.

1. Your Bible study group should have a leader, whose task it is to make the sessions interesting, clear and practical. The leader should determine how much of each lesson in the manual should be studied each time (some lessons, because of the material covered, may be broken down into smaller units). He should lead the discussions (or assign discussion leaders) and encourage the doing of homework assignments which he might give.

2. Get in the good habit of using pencil and paper freely in all your study. Record your observations as you read the Bible passage of the lesson. Do not hesitate to make small notations (e.g., underlining a key word or phrase) in your Bible. A pencil is one of your best eyes! Write out answers to questions in the manual. Write out questions that come to you as you study at home, and ask these when your group comes together.

3. Read all the Bible references cited in the manual. There is no substitute for letting the Bible speak for itself.

4. Do not rush through the preparatory Lessons 1 and 2. Your analysis of the actual Bible text, beginning with Lesson 3, will be more fruitful if you first learn well the "language" of these Bible books.

5. Study carefully the charts and diagrams in the lessons. This writer has included in all the books of this self-study series many such visual aids, because he is convinced that such eye-gate devices are effective helps for clarification, impression, methodicalness, and context orientation. Survey charts give an overview of the Bible book or section, so that you will be aware of the surrounding context in the Bible. Historical charts furnish the setting of the Bible book. Analytical charts provide a work sheet on which to record one's observations and outlines of a particular passage.

In group study it is very helpful to have large reproductions of the charts (e.g., on chalkboard or paper) in full view of everyone for the frequent references to context or setting which arise when studying Bible books like these. The use of overhead projectors for displaying charts in group study is highly recommended.

4

GEOGRAPHY OF EZRA—NEHEMIAH—ESTHER   SHOWING ROUTE OF RETURNING EXILES   Chart B

LIMITS OF PERSIAN EMPIRE (c. 500 B.C.) ....

6. Include these in all group study:

a. At the beginning of the hour *review* the previous lesson.

b. Everyone should be encouraged to *participate* in discussion, including the asking of *any kind* of question related to the lesson.

c. Keep looking for everyday *applications* of the Bible text. Someone has written, "To look is one thing. To see what you look at is another. To understand what you see is a third. To learn from what you understand is still something else. But to act on what you learn is what really matters."

d. At the end of the hour *summarize* the highlights of the lesson.

7. Let a dependence on the Holy Spirit underlie all your Bible study. He who inspired the writers of the Scriptures wants to enlighten you as a student of those Scriptures, to bring forth eternal fruit in your life. (Read John 16:12-15 and I Cor. 2:12-13.)

Historical Setting of Ezra, Nehemiah and Esther

A DEEPER APPRECIATION AND UNDERSTANDING

OF EZRA, NEHEMIAH AND ESTHER ARE

GAINED FROM THEIR HISTORICAL SETTING.

This lesson therefore is devoted to such a background study. As you read the lesson try to visualize places, persons and events. Master this first lesson and you will feel more at home with the Bible text of the three books to be studied in the lessons that follow.

I. THE TWO CAPTIVITIES.

When we speak of "restoration" in Ezra's day we are referring to the *return* of God's people to Canaan *from captivity*. That captivity took place in two stages, which are known as the Assyrian and Babylonian captivities (see Chart C).

THE TWO CAPTIVITIES   **Chart C**

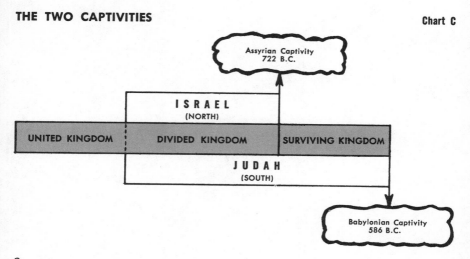

A. Assyrian Captivity (fall of Samaria, 722 B.C., recorded in II Kings 17).

Most of the people and rulers of the ten tribes of the northern kingdom of Israel were deported to Assyria and scattered among the inhabitants there. (Locate Assyria on Chart B.) *Zondervan Pictorial Bible Dictionary* comments on what happened to these people and their offspring in the years that followed:

> The Ten Tribes taken into captivity, sometimes called the Lost Tribes of Israel, must not be thought of as being absorbed by the peoples among whom they settled. Some undoubtedly were, but many others retained their Israelitish religion and traditions. Some became part of the Jewish dispersion, and others very likely returned with the exiles of Judah who had been carried off by Nebuchadnezzar.*

B. Babylonian Captivity (fall of Jerusalem, 586 B.C., recorded in II Kings 25).

The fall of Jerusalem in 586 B.C. sealed the fate of the two tribes of the southern kingdom of Judah. Nebuchadnezzar was the captor, and Babylon was the place of exile. Second Kings closes with an account of this tragic event in Judah's history. Read this chapter at this time to appreciate the theme of the restoration books.

Note: Unless otherwise stated, the names "Israel" and "Judah," denoting the chosen people of God, will be used interchangeably throughout this manual.

II. DURATION OF THE BABYLONIAN CAPTIVITY.

Before Judah was taken captive, Jeremiah had prophesied that the duration of exile would be seventy years† (read Jer. 25:11-12; 29:10; II Chron. 36:21). The exile began with Nebuchadnezzar's first invasion of Judah in 605 B.C. (II Chron. 36:2-7), and ended with the first return of the Jews to Canaan in 536 B.C.‡ (Ezra 1). See Chart D.§

° Merrill C. Tenney (ed.), *Zondervan Pictorial Bible Dictionary*, p. 147.

† The number 70 may have been a round number, as is often the case in Scripture.

‡ If Jeremiah's prophecy is interpreted from an ecclesiastical standpoint, with the temple as the key object, then the 70-year period extended from the destruction of the temple in 586 B.C. to the year of completion of its reconstruction, which was 516 B.C.

§ Most of the dates of Chart D are those of John C. Whitcomb's chart in *Old Testament Kings and Prophets*.

HISTORICAL SETTING OF EZRA—NEHEMIAH—ESTHER

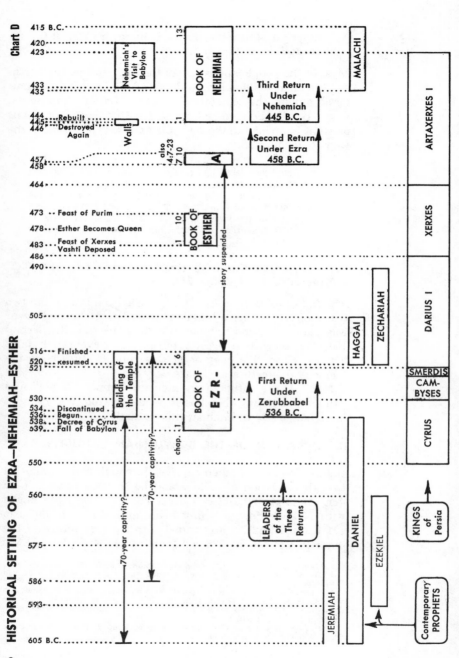

8

III. CONTEMPORARY RULERS.

The Jews in exile in Babylonia were subject to the kings of the Neo-Babylonian Empire, such as Nebuchadnezzar. When Cyrus, king of Persia, overthrew Babylon in 539 B.C., the rule of Babylonia was transferred to the Persian Empire. Cyrus' policy of liberation for the exiles in Babylonia brought about the first return of Jewish exiles to the land of their fathers. Observe on Chart D the names of the Persian kings who succeeded Cyrus. The names of Darius and Artaxerxes appear frequently in the books of Ezra and Nehemiah (observe this in an exhaustive Bible concordance).

IV. LEADERS OF THE RESTORATION.

The three key leaders of the returning Jews were Zerubbabel, Ezra and Nehemiah. Zerubbabel and Nehemiah were appointed by Cyrus and Artaxerxes, respectively, as governors of the Jewish returnees. Ezra was a leading priest of the Jews who not only was leader of the second return but also was a co-worker with Nehemiah on the third. Locate the names of Zerubbabel,|| Ezra and Nehemiah on Chart D. Note also the dates associated with each of the three returns to Judah:

536 B.C. First return—under Zerubbabel

458 B.C. Second return—under Ezra

445 B.C. Third return#—under Nehemiah

Fix in your mind the other dates and events cited on the chart.

The preaching and teaching ministries of three prophets during the restoration period should not be overlooked. Observe on Chart D when Haggai, Zechariah and Malachi ministered. Read Ezra 5:1 and 6:14 for brief but important mention of the influence of Haggai and Zechariah. The name Malachi does not appear in these or any other historical books. Observe on the chart that most of Malachi's ministry took place during Nehemiah's return visit to Babylon. Those were years of backsliding on the part of the Jews in Canaan, when the first spiritual zeal had subsided. Hence the message of Malachi was mainly about sin and its judgment.

|| Zerubbabel is probably the Sheshbazzar referred to in Ezra 1:8, 11.
\# No large contingent of Jews was involved in this return.

The Prophet Daniel went into exile with the first contingent of Jews in 605 B.C., and was ministering in Babylon in the service of Darius the Mede (who was made king of Babylon by Cyrus, Dan. 5:31; 9:1) when the exiles received permission to return (cf. Dan. 1:21; 6:28). Though aged Daniel did not return to Jerusalem with the exiles, he supported the project in spirit (see Dan. 9:1 ff.).

V. COVERAGE OF THE BIBLE BOOKS.

Observe on Chart D the periods covered by each of the three books of Ezra, Nehemiah and Esther. Note the suspension of the story of Ezra for a number of years. Note also that Esther chronologically fits between chapters 6 and 7 of Ezra, during the reign of Xerxes.

VI. IMPORTANCE OF THE RESTORATION FOR THE JEWS AND THE WORLD.

The restoration was important for various reasons. For Israel, it showed that God had not forgotten His promise to Abraham concerning the land of Canaan (e.g., read Gen. 13:15 and note the strength of the phrase "for ever"). Hence the *relocation* of a returning remnant. Hope for a missionary outreach to Gentiles was stirred up in the *revival* of true worship, for a key mission of Israel was to show heathen nations of the world what true worship of the true God was. And then, the restoration was directly related to the life and ministry of the coming Messiah, in the *renewal* of the Messianic promises. For example, Bethlehem, Nazareth and Zion were some of the geographical places woven into the promises concerning Jesus' coming. In about four hundred years Jesus would be born of the seed of David in *Bethlehem, not* in Babylon. The Holy Land of *promise, not* a land of captivity, was where His people would be dwelling when He would come unto them, "his own" (John 1:11).

*   *   *

Some Review Questions

1. Name the two captivities of God's people in Old Testament times._____

_____

Identify the captive groups, the captors, dates, and places of exile._____

_____

_____

_____

2.   Name one major prophet who foretold coming captivity for Judah._____

3.   How long was the Babylonian captivity?_____
What are two possible interpretations as to when the period

began and ended?_____

_____

4.   How many main returns to Canaan were there?_____

Name the Jewish leaders and dates of each return._____

_____

5.   Below are listed the major Persian kings from 550 to 423 B.C. See how much you can recall of Chart D as you record in the space below such things as names of leaders and prophets, events, and the periods covered by the three books of Ezra, Nehemiah and Esther.

550 B.C.	530	521		486	464	423 B.C.
CYRUS			DARIUS I	XERXES	ARTAXERXES I	

6. What are some of the big truths taught about God and about man from each of the two crucial events in Israel's history shown below? Ponder this carefully, and record your answers:

	The Captivities	The Restoration
Truths about God		
Truths about man		

BOOK OF EZRA
Background and Survey
of Ezra

THE BOOK OF EZRA SHINES FORTH IN

VIVID CONTRAST TO THE BOOK IT

FOLLOWS IN THE BIBLE, II CHRONICLES.

Surely no darker words are found in Scripture than those of the last chapter of II Chronicles. The chronicler (who may have been Ezra) there speaks of the people and leaders spurning the compassionate entreaties of God by hardening their hearts, polluting the temple, and mocking God's messengers, to the point where "there was no remedy" (II Chron. 36:16). What tragedy in those words! Israel's judgment of exile in Babylon was inevitable and just. If there would be restoration of any sort, it would be totally of God's grace. This is the bright message of Ezra to which we now turn our attention.

I. BACKGROUND.

A. Title of Book and Place in the Canon.

The book of Ezra is named after its principal character. (If Ezra was its author, this would also account for the title.) Actually the name Ezra does not appear in the story until 7:1, but he still may be regarded as the key person in the book.

In our English Bible Ezra follows II Chronicles, picking up the story where II Chronicles leaves it (cf. II Chron. 36:22-23; Ezra 1:1-3). In the Hebrew canon Ezra and Nehemiah were considered as one historical book,* and were located just before Chronicles.

* The first division into two books in the Hebrew Bible was made in A.D. 1448.

13

B. Date and Authorship.

The traditional view is that Ezra wrote the book which bears his name. If he also wrote I and II Chronicles, which is very possible, then we have in these three books a continuous historical record by the one author. (Compare the third- and first-person references to Ezra in such verses as 7:1, 11, 25, 28; 8:15, 16, 17, 21.)

Ezra may have written this book soon after he arrived in Jerusalem (458 B.C.), around 450 B.C.

C. The Man Ezra.

Ezra has always been considered a key figure in Jewish history. Just as Moses led Israel from Egypt to Canaan, Ezra led the Jews from Babylon to the land of their fathers. Ezra's name means "helper" (from the Hebrew *'ezer,* "help"), and helper of his people he truly was. He ministered to his fellow Jews in captivity, and he led a group of them back to Jerusalem in 458 B.C. When Nehemiah arrived in Jerusalem thirteen years later, Ezra helped him in ministering to the people about spiritual matters (cf. Neh. 8:9).

Ezra is referred to in the Bible as a priest and scribe (e.g., Ezra 7:6, 21).† One of his key ministries was to revive the people's interest in the Scriptures. Some believe that Ezra was the author of Psalm 119, the great "Word" psalm. In any case, he loved the Word and loved to teach it.

Hebrew tradition says that Ezra served in Babylon as a high priest, that he originated the Jewish-synagogue form of worship, and collected the Old Testament books into a unit. Read Ezra 7:1-5 and observe that Ezra was a descendant of Aaron, the high priest of Moses' day.

D. Historical Background.

Read 1:1; 4:5, 24 and 7:1 for the references to three important kings of Persia: Cyrus, Darius, Artaxerxes.‡ You will recall these names from your study of Chart D. How the account of Ezra proceeds chronologically with reference to these kings is shown on Chart E.

---

† The phrase "ready scribe" (Ezra 7:6) is translated by the Berkeley Version as "scribe, well versed."

‡ The references to Ahasuerus (Xerxes) and Artaxerxes in 4:6-7 are part of the parenthesis 4:6-23, inserted out of chronological order with a purpose.

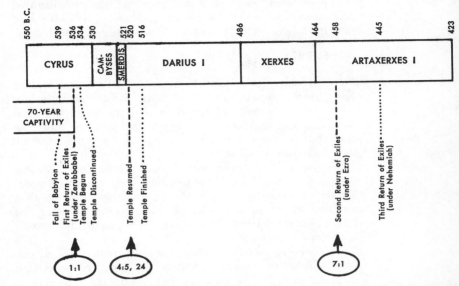

It can be seen from Chart D how Ezra is not a continuous or complete historical record of any one period, but follows the principle of selectivity. For example, Ezra passes over the period from the completion of the temple (516 B.C.) to his own journey to Jerusalem (458 B.C.). Bible authors were inspired to select only those materials of the historical record which have a bearing on the subject being discussed. This should always be kept in mind when studying Bible history. (It may be observed here also that the two books of Ezra and Nehemiah contain practically all that is known of the history of the Jews between 538 and about 425 B.C.)

E. Purposes of the Book of Ezra.

The book of Ezra shows how the Lord fulfilled His promises, given through His prophets, to restore Israel to their own land.§ He moved heathen monarchs to show favor to the Jews, and raised up leaders (Zerubbabel and Ezra) and prophets (Haggai and Zechariah) for the grand task of restoration. The restoration involved the physical aspect

§ Isaiah prophesied concerning Cyrus 200 years before Cyrus was born (read Isa. 44:28; 45:1-4). For Jeremiah's prophecy, read Jer. 25:11-12; 29:10.

—moving back to Canaan and rebuilding the temple buildings; and, more vital, the spiritual aspect—restoring true worship, reestablishing the authority of God's law, and initiating reforms in the everyday life of the Jews.

II. SURVEY.

Now we should be ready to come to the biblical text of Ezra. In our study thus far we have acquainted ourselves with the background of the book of Ezra, involving such things as people, places and events. In a sense it might be said that we have learned the language of Ezra; now we can study the book itself.

Survey is the skyscraper view of large and general things in a book; analysis is the close scrutiny of the smaller details. Survey should always be made first so that analysis of small parts can be made in the light of the larger context. "Image the whole, then execute the parts" is the rule of study here.

To make a survey of Ezra we must read through the book without interruption at least one time. The procedure recommended below involves two readings: the first, a quick scanning, and the second, a closer view.

A. First Reading.

Your first reading should only be a scanning of the book of Ezra, observing such things as number of chapters, length of chapters and type of content. Concerning content, how much of the following is found in Ezra?

action _____

conversation _____

description _____

listings _____

letters _____

prayers _____

Mark your Bible wherever blocks of the last three types appear.

B. Second Reading.

Spend a little more time on this second reading of Ezra, but do not get bogged down in details. Remember, analysis comes *after* survey.

Read the book chapter by chapter. That is, become aware of the reasons for a *new* chapter as the book progresses. If your Bible shows paragraph divisions in its text,|| your scanning of chapters will be made a lot easier.

Record the main theme of each chapter:

1.

2.

3.

4.

5.

6.

7.

8.

9.

10.

Next record a chapter title (one to three words) on Chart F. Chapter titles usually reflect something of the main theme of the chapter. They are not intended to form an outline of the book.

UNCOMPLETED SURVEY CHART OF EZRA Chart F

Use these spaces for outlines of the book:

|| American Standard Version and Berkeley Version are two such Bibles.

Use Chart F as a work sheet to record other observations as you make them in the course of your study. Some of the study questions given below may suggest things you will want to record on the chart.

1. What are some of your first impressions of the book of Ezra?_____

_____

2. What are some repeated words and phrases of Ezra?

_____

_____

3. Where are references made to kings? Mark these places in your Bible. Mark also in your Bible the letters recorded in Ezra._____

_____

4. Compare the beginning and end of the book._____

Does the introduction introduce, and does the conclusion conclude? Does your answer to the latter question explain, at least in part, why Ezra-Nehemiah was treated as one book in the Hebrew Bible? Could 10:18-44 be considered an appendix to the book?_____

5. Where is the first appearance of the man Ezra in the book? _____

Who is the leader mentioned in 2:2a?_____

How often does he appear in chapters 1—6?_____

Does he appear in chapters 7—10? (An exhaustive concordance will quickly answer this.)_____

6. Record on Chart F outlines for the following subjects:
a. Main subject of chapters 1—6 and of chapters 7—10.
b. Main subject of chapters 1—2; 3—6; 7—8; 9—10.

7.   Where is the decree of Cyrus recorded?_____

The first journey to Canaan?_____

The decree of Artaxerxes?_____

The second journey?_____

_____

8.   In your own words, what is the main theme of Ezra?

_____

_____

_____

As you continue your study of Ezra, be on the lookout for a key verse that suggests such a theme.

III.   A SURVEY CHART OF EZRA.

After you have completed your own independent study in the areas suggested above, examine the survey which is diagrammed on Chart G.

Observe the following on the chart:

1.   The ten chapters of Ezra are divided into two main parts, with 7:1 beginning the new section.

2.   The first section concerns the first return of exiles under the leadership of Governor Zerubbabel; the second section is about the second return, under the leadership of Priest Ezra. How many years elapsed between the two returns?   _____

_____

3.   The main work accomplished on the first return was the rebuilding of the temple. On the second return Ezra's main task was to bring his people to a place of repentance, confession of sin, and restitution, so that true worship of God could be restored. The sin of mixed marriages (between Israelites and the heathen) was a major defilement at this time. How did this sin affect the religious life of Israel?

_____

4.   Observe from the dates shown on the chart the duration of the time between chapters 6 and 7. Consult Chart D and note that the book of Esther is located in this period.

EZRA   RESTORATION AND REFORM

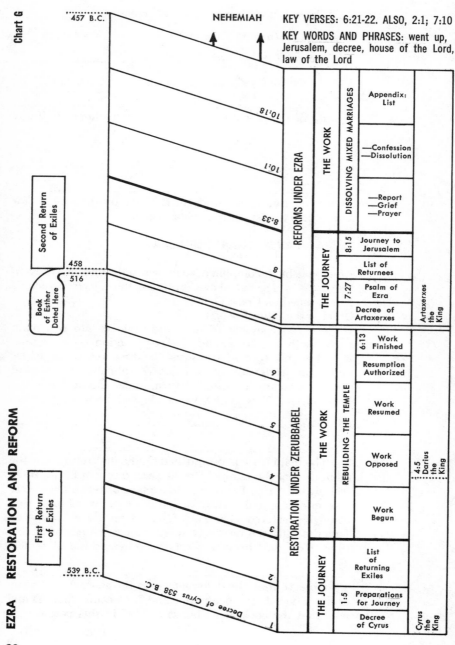

NEHEMIAH

KEY VERSES: 6:21-22. ALSO, 2:1; 7:10

KEY WORDS AND PHRASES: went up, Jerusalem, decree, house of the Lord, law of the Lord

457 B.C.

Second Return of Exiles

First Return of Exiles

Book of Esther Dated Here

458
516

539 B.C.

Decree of Cyrus 538 B.C.

REFORMS UNDER EZRA

THE WORK — DISSOLVING MIXED MARRIAGES
- Appendix: List
- —Confession
- —Dissolution
- —Report
- —Grief
- —Prayer

10:18
10:1
8:33

THE JOURNEY
- 8:15 Journey to Jerusalem
- List of Returnees
- 7:27 Psalm of Ezra
- Decree of Artaxerxes

8
7

Artaxerxes the King

RESTORATION UNDER ZERUBBABEL

THE WORK — REBUILDING THE TEMPLE
- 6:13 Work Finished
- Resumption Authorized
- Work Resumed
- Work Opposed
- Work Begun

6
5
4
3

4:5 Darius the King

THE JOURNEY
- List of Returning Exiles
- 1:5 Preparations for Journey
- Decree of Cyrus

2
1

Cyrus the King

5. The names of the three important kings of Persia—Cyrus, Darius and Artaxerxes—are placed on the chart where they relate to the story.

6. In chapters 4—7 Ezra records much of the official correspondence involving the kings' offices and having to do with the Jews' permission to return to Canaan. Originally these letters were written in Aramaic, which was the official language of diplomatic intercourse in those days. Ezra preserved the letters in their original Aramaic form. This is one of the few Aramaic sections in the Hebrew Bible. Identify the sender and addressee in each case:

4:11-16 _____

4:17-22 _____

5:7-17 _____

6:6-12 _____

7:11-26 _____

7. Some key words and phrases of Ezra are: "went up," "Jerusalem," "decree," "house of the Lord," "hand of the Lord upon him," "law of the Lord." The Word of God is prominent throughout the book, under various designations. Look up each verse cited here and jot down the word or phrase used:

1:1	7:10
3:2	7:14
6:14	9:4
6:18	10:3,5
7:6	

8. A suggested key sentence in Ezra is 6:21-22. Two other verses which might be called key verses are 2:1 and 7:10.
9. Chart G shows a title we are using for Ezra, reflecting the outline of the book: "Restoration and Reform." Try making your own title.

A Concluding Exercise

In this lesson you have learned much about the background of the book of Ezra, and you have made a survey study of the book in general. You have no doubt already seen some prominent spiritual lessons taught by the book. For a concluding exercise, list such lessons related to the areas of truth shown below. You will have more opportunity to expand on this exercise in the lessons that follow.

AREA OF TRUTH	SPIRITUAL LESSONS
God's grace	
God's holiness	
God's promises	
God's sovereignty	
Service for God	
Leadership	
Prayer	

First Return of the Exiles

ONE OF THE BRIGHTER DAYS IN JEREMIAH'S

MINISTRY WAS WHEN HE WROTE A LETTER

TO THE JEWISH EXILES IN BABYLON.

He reminded them that God would lead His people back to Canaan at the end of seventy years. "After seventy years be accomplished at Babylon I [the Lord] will visit you, and perform my good work toward you, in causing you to return to this place" (Jer. 29:10). Although most of the exiles reading the letter would die in the meantime because of age, they had the consolation that their children would experience the happy privilege of returning "home."

Now the time of deliverance had arrived. After Cyrus, king of Persia, conquered Babylon in 539 B.C., he issued the decree permitting (and encouraging) the Jews to return to the land of their fathers. The decree, preparations for the journey, and a list of the returning exiles make up the record of the passage which we shall now study.

I. PREPARATION FOR STUDY.

As a preparation for your analysis, do the following:

1. Read Jeremiah 29—Jeremiah's letter to the exiles.

2. Read Isaiah 44:28; 45:1-4, 7, 13—Isaiah's prophecy concerning Cyrus.

3. Read Daniel 9. Daniel prayed this prayer in the year Cyrus conquered Babylon (539 B.C.). Observe his concern for Jerusalem and the temple (e.g., 9:16-19). God's answer to Daniel, in the form of vision, not only promised restoration (9:25) but the coming of the Messiah in the last days (9:25-27).

4. Read II Chronicles 36:22-23. If Ezra wrote the books of Chronicles and Ezra, this was his device to show a continuity.

5. Review Chart D.

II. ANALYSIS.

This passage is of three parts:

First Return of Exiles in 536 B.C.		
1:1	1:5	2:1 2:70
Decree of Cyrus	Preparations for the Journey	List of Returning Exiles

Most of your analysis should be concentrated on chapter 1.

A. Decree of Cyrus (1:1-4).

1. Read the paragraph carefully. The phrase "in the first year" (v. 1) refers to the year in which Cyrus conquered Babylon, or 539 B.C. Compare the phrases "word of the LORD" and "mouth of Jeremiah" (v. 1). What is taught here about fulfillment of prophecy?_____

_____

Observe that the Lord moved in the heart of a secular ruler (v.1). Do you think the Lord does the same today?

_____

2. Compare the ways Cyrus refers to God in the decree (vv. 2-4)._____

_____

_____

Does Cyrus claim God to be his personal God?_____

_____

3. Derive some spiritual lessons from this group of phrases in verse 3:

"Who is there among you?"_____

"His God be with him"_____

"Let him go up"_____

4. Compare Cyrus' sense of obligation ("God . . . hath *given me . . . charged me*") with the voluntary quality of

the invitation-permission of verses 3-4._____

_____

B. Preparations for the Journey (1:5-11).
1.   What do you learn from verses 5 and 6 about response to a call; God's work in bringing a response; and voluntary offering? _____

_____

_____

2.   What good quality of Cyrus appears in verses 7 and 8?

_____

3.   Note: The name "Sheshbazzar" (v. 8) was probably the Babylonian name for "Zerubbabel" (2:2; cf. 5:14, 16).

C.   List of Returning Exiles (2:1-70; scan Neh. 7:5-73 for a similar list).
Observe these phrases in the opening and closing verses: "came again unto Jerusalem and Judah, every one unto his city" (v. 1); "So . . . all Israel [dwelt] in their cities" (v. 70).

Note the prominent place given to the holy city, and to the fact that the return involved the *whole* land of Judah. This was not merely a *token* return, even though more Jews remained behind in Babylon than chose to return.

The list is arranged in the Bible text in an orderly fashion:

Leaders: Zerubbabel (mentioned first because he was highest in authority) and his associates* (2:2)

People: 1. identified by families (2:2*b*-19)
            2. identified by towns in Palestine (2:20-35)

Religious leaders: 1. priests (2:36-39)—these only could serve at the altar
                       2. Levites (2:40-42)—mainly religious instructors

Servants: 1. Nethinim (2:43-54)—these served the Levites (8:20)
              2. descendants of Solomon's servants

Those of uncertain genealogy: (2:59-63)

* Observe that the name "Sheshbazzar" of 1:8, 11 does not appear in this list, which supports the view that Sheshbazzar and Zerubbabel are one and the same man.

Let the above listing help form an image of the group (around 50,000) that returned to Judah at this time. Observe the small numbers of Levites who chose to return (cf. 8:15 for the same problem during the second return). What may have been the reason for this?_____

_____

Read Matthew 1:12 and observe that Zerubbabel was an ancestor of Joseph. How significant was this?_____

_____

Study the phrases of 2:68. What are your observations?

_____

For group discussion, consider the phrase "house of God." You will find this a very profitable experience.

III. COMMENTS.

1. We don't usually think of God using secular powers, such as Cyrus, to be His voice to His people when the occasion arises. Should we not remember that God is sovereign Lord of history, not only setting the stage and controlling its action, but also using its actors *as He will*? One important lesson is taught by this—that as believers we need to be sensitive to the Spirit's voice however it may reach us.

2. Only a minority of Jews in exile (about 50,000) chose to return to their fathers' homeland at this time. Read Jeremiah 29:4-7 to understand why it was not a hard decision for many Jews to *remain* in Babylon. What do you think was the motivation of the returnees? Where did this "drive" originate? (Cf. 1:5.)

IV. CONCLUSION.

The "house of the LORD" (2:68), the holy city of Jerusalem (2:68) and cities for the people's dwellings (2:70) were the three goals of the returning Jews, in that order of importance. As we move into the next chapter (chap. 3) of Ezra, we will observe how top priority was given to the reconstruction of the house of the Lord.

Restoration
of Public Worship

AT THE CLOSE OF THE LAST LESSON,

ALL ISRAEL DWELT IN THEIR CITIES;

THE JOURNEY BACK TO CANAAN WAS A SUCCESS.

We also saw in the lesson that the Israelites at that time recognized the priority which must be given to the worship of God in His house (2:68). Chapters 3 to 6 now describe the project of rebuilding this house, the temple of God, and the problems involved.

To appreciate something of the emotion involved as the Jews anticipated erecting their temple again, read Psalm 122, which describes the exultation of a soul who loves the house of the Lord.

I.   ANALYSIS.

Four segments comprise this lesson* (a segment is a group of paragraphs). See Chart G to identify what these segments are. Before studying each segment separately, read chapters 3—6 at one time to feel the movement of the story. Compare the beginning of the story (3:1-7) with the end (e.g., 6:16-22). Observe the words "Consecration" and "Dedication" on Chart H.

Chart H is a work sheet of the four segments, to be used for recording your observations. For more working space, transfer the analytical charts to large paper. Some observations are already recorded on Chart H as a starter. Let these be suggestions of the types of observations which you can record on the analytical charts.

* The lesson could be studied in four separate units, if desired.

REBUILDING THE TEMPLE
Ezra 3:1—6:22

Chart H

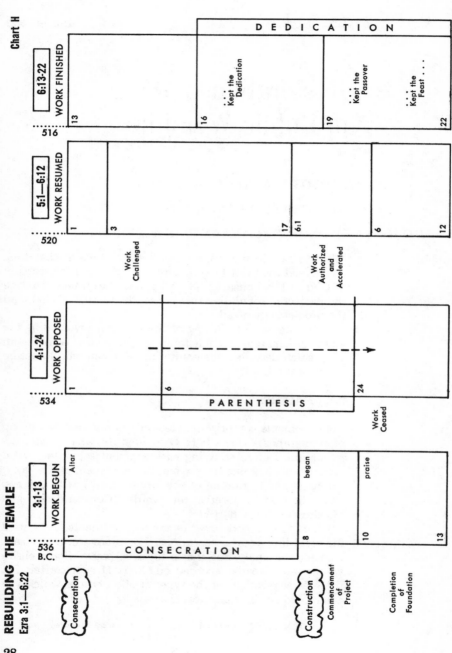

3:1-13	4:1-24	5:1—6:12	6:13-22
WORK BEGUN	WORK OPPOSED	WORK RESUMED	WORK FINISHED

536 B.C.
534
520
516

3:1-13 WORK BEGUN

Altar
began
praise

1
8
10
13

CONSECRATION

Consecration

Construction
Commencement of Project

Completion of Foundation

4:1-24 WORK OPPOSED

1
6
24

PARENTHESIS

Work Ceased

5:1—6:12 WORK RESUMED

1
3
17
6:1
6
12

Work Challenged

Work Authorized and Accelerated

6:13-22 WORK FINISHED

DEDICATION

13
16
19
22

Kept the Dedication

Kept the Passover

Kept the Feast . . .

1.   Read 3:1-7. What is the theme of this paragraph?___

_____

Observe the progression, in the following sequence, from the general to the specific:

"cities"

"Jerusalem"

"altar"

(v. 1)

(v. 1)

(v. 2)   (also "temple," v. 6)

Where does this progression focus the attention?

_____

2.   What spiritual truths are taught by these key words in the paragraph: altar, law, feast?_____

_____

_____

_____

3.   What is the impact of verse 6b, beginning with the word "But"?_____

_____

4.   Read 3:8-9. A key word here is "began" (v. 8).†
What was begun?_____

_____

Why are beginnings and foundations so important for any project, ministry or career?_____

_____

_____

5.   Read 3:10-13. What project was completed here?_____

_____

† The grammar of v. 8 in the King James Version is insufficient. See Berkeley or Revised Standard Version.

What is the tone of this paragraph?_____

_____

What were two causes for praise, according to verse 11?
Record this on your work sheet.

Account for the weeping of verse 12._____

_____

Observe here the encounter between the old generation and
the new. Does verse 13 intend to teach a spiritual truth?

_____

Can the old and new generations today work together in

the church's task of evangelization? If so, how?_____

_____

_____

_____

_____

DATELINES OF THE TEMPLE AND WALLS PROJECT   Chart I

550 B.C.	536 534	530	521 520 516		486	464	446 444	423 B.C.
CYRUS	CAM-BYSES	SMERDIS	DARIUS		XERXES		ARTAXERXES	

Temple Begun / Temple Discontinued

Temple Resumed / Temple Finished

Walls of Jerusalem Destroyed Again / Walls Rebuilt

3:8 ⌐   4:24 ⌐   ⌐6:15   DATE-LINES   (4:23)⌐   ⌐Neh. 2:1

Main Core	Parenthesis
EZRA 4:1-5, 24	4:6-23

30

B. The Work Opposed (4:1-24).

This is the chapter that records the discontinuation of the temple project. Read the datelines in the Bible references shown on Chart I. Observe also the years covered by the two parts of Ezra 4.

1. Read the "Main Core" of chapter 4 (4:1-5, 24), referring to Chart I as you read. Keep in mind that the "adversaries" (v. 1) were Samaritans, or "half Jews," offspring of the marriage of foreigners and Israelites after the northern tribes were taken captive (II Kings 17:24). What are the two kinds of opposition recorded here?_____

_____

Why did the Israelites‡ refuse the offer of help?_____

_____

Did the words "We seek your God" (v. 2) represent a quest for salvation? Study the Jews' reply of verse 3 as to

_____

why they did not accept the offer of help. Note that they said, "We . . . will build . . . as king Cyrus . . . hath commanded us." Now read the wording of his commandment (1:2-4) and note that only Jews were commissioned to do the work.

Think about the meaning of these strong words: "adversaries" (v. 1); "weakened," "troubled" (v. 4); "frustrate" (v. 5). What spiritual lessons are taught in these verses?

_____

_____

_____

2. Now read the parenthesis of 4:6-23. Why did the author insert this here?_____

_____

What does this add to the story of Israel's trial?_____

_____

‡ In 4:1 the Israelites are represented as "Judah and Benjamin," because most of the returning exiles were of these two tribes, settling down in those regions.

Why did Artaxerxes give the order that the temple project be halted? _____

_____

_____

C. The Work Resumed (5:1—6:12).

For how many years was the temple project halted? (Chart I). _____

Read Haggai 1 (which is dated 520 B.C.) and observe that one evil effect of the discontinuation of the temple building was that the Jews themselves had lost their original zeal for the project. Then when the work was finally resumed (described in our present passage) it was not without a challenge from new adversaries, from outside.

1. Read 5:1-2. According to verse 1 what part did the prophets play in the new work? (You have already read Hag. 1; now read Zech. 1:1-7 to learn more of the message of the prophets.) Does Ezra 5:2b suggest another kind of help given by the prophets?_____

_____

2. Read 5:3—6:5. (Note: 5:4 is better translated thus: "Then we told them after this manner, what the names of the men were that were making this building," ASV. (Cf. 5:9-10. The geographical location of "on this side the river" was the west side of the Euphrates River.) What evidences of God's help appear in this passage, either explicit or implied?_____

_____

3. Read 6:6-12. Darius not only authorized the temple project; he financed part of it and urged its speedy completion. Read 6:22 to learn God's part in this.

D. The Work Finished (6:13-22).

1. Read 6:13-15. Record the part each of the following played in the project:

Tatnai: _____

elders: _____

prophets: _____

God: _____

Cyrus, Darius, and Artaxerxes:§_____

2. Read 6:16-22. According to the previous paragraph, the house of the Lord was completed. What is the spiritual significance of a dedication when a project is completed or a goal attained? What ceremonies were observed at the

dedication of the temple?_____

_____

_____

(Observe the repetition of the word "kept.") These ceremonies had originated a thousand years earlier, during the time of the exodus of Israel from Egypt. Read about each of these to sense the innermost feelings of the Jews on this holy dedication day:

Sin Offering (6:17): Leviticus 16:1-28
Passover (6:19): Exodus 12:43-50; Leviticus 23:5
Feast of Unleavened Bread (6:22): Leviticus 23:6-8

II. COMMENTS.

1. The foundation project of the temple was as important as that of the superstructure itself, calling for a service of praise (3:10-11). In the case of the invisible church, the body of Christ, the foundation is even greater than the structure, for the foundation is Christ Himself (I Cor. 3:11).

2. The two reactions of 3:12-13 are interesting. The older people remembered the exquisite beauties of Solomon's temple, now destroyed, and so they could only weep as they were reminded of a glory which was only a memory. The younger generation shouted for joy, for they never had a temple before this. So there were two reactions, and thus a confusion of noise, but the text does not say that a division arose. All the people were of one mind: here in the new temple they would worship the God of their fathers.

3. Whenever there is progress in God's work, the adver-

§ Concerning the inclusion of this later king, *The Wycliffe Bible Commentary*, p. 429, notes, "Ezra is careful to add the name of his own king, Artaxerxes, because he helped in the maintenance of the Temple (7:15, 16, 21)."

sary, Satan|| himself, sends opposition. The opposition may come subtly, slowly and indirectly, or it may come openly, quickly and directly. But it comes, and as Christians we need to be vigilant concerning this adversary of our soul (read I Peter 5:8-9).

4. "And with them were the prophets of God helping them" (5:2). Part of the prophets' ministry was prophesying and teaching, but no small part must have been that of inspiring (and maybe even physical assistance), suggested by the word "helping."

III. CONCLUSION.

The last two verses of the passage of this lesson could be called key verses for Ezra. They summarize the first return of Jewish exiles from captivity in 536 B.C., with the aid of God and through the favor of an Assyrian king (6:21-22). When the core is extracted from these verses, a bright note of gladness is the emphasized concluding message: "The children of Israel . . . did eat . . . with joy: for the LORD had made them joyful."

|| Both the Hebrew and Greek words for Satan mean literally "adversary."

Second Return of the Exiles, and Reforms Under Ezra

ABOUT SIXTY YEARS TRANSPIRED BETWEEN
CHAPTERS 6 AND 7, PROBABLY YEARS OF
SPIRITUAL DECLINE FOR JEWS IN JUDAH.

Surely the coming of Ezra the scribe with a second contingent of returning exiles was very timely, for Ezra was a man of God who had a heavy burden to teach Israel the "statutes and judgments" of God (read 7:10). So his ministry was bound to touch not only the lives of those making the journey with him, but also the lives of those already in the land.

The story of the book of Esther fits chronologically between chapters 6 and 7 of Ezra. The divine providence shown to the Jews during the reign of Xerxes, predecessor of Artaxerxes, may have influenced Artaxerxes to show favor to the Jews during his reign, such as encouraging them to return to their homeland (7:11-26).

I. REVIEW.

This would be a good time in your study of Ezra to review the survey chart of the book (Chart G). Recall that the book is divided into two main parts: "Restoration Under Zerubbabel" and "Reforms Under Ezra." Ezra the man does not play a part in the story of the book in the first six chapters. Now at 7:1 he appears, and remains as the main character to the end of the book.*

The story of chapters 7 to 10 may be divided into two main parts: "The Journey" and "The Work." Chart J is a

---

* In 7:1-26 and chap. 10 the reference to Ezra is in the third person (e.g., 7:6); in 7:27—9:15 the reference is in the first person (e.g., 8:1). This interchanging style of narration was often used by writers in Ezra's day, and is not an argument against authorship of the whole book by Ezra.

survey of this passage which we will be studying in this lesson. Single words are chosen for the smaller parts of the outline to aid in remembering the progression of ·the story. Try making your own outline of these chapters, recording it on a chart similar to this. (Note: The lesson may be broken down into smaller units of study if desired.)

EZRA 7:1—10:44   Chart J

7:1 REFORMS UNDER EZRA									10:44
The Journey				The Work					
	7:27	8:1	8:15	DISSOLUTION OF MIXED MARRIAGES					
					9:1	9:5	10:1	10:5	10:18
Permission	Psalm	People	Pilgrimage	Problem	Program	Prayer	Penitence	Pro-pitiation	Appendix List of Guilty Ones

II. ANALYSIS.

A. The Journey (7:1—8:32).

Just as foreign kings of heathen religions sent God's people into captivity, so foreign kings sponsored the three returns of the Jews to their homeland. Zerubbabel was the officially appointed leader of the first return; Ezra led the second; and Nehemiah, the third.† Our present study concerns the second return (458 B.C.).

1. THE PERMISSION (7:1-26). The first ten verses of chapter 7 introduce the story of these chapters. Read the verses, observing what is said about each of these subjects (record your observations):

---

† Actually the third group did not comprise a large contingent of Jews, but rather a company of leaders and workers. It is interesting to observe that God chose men of differing backgrounds to be the leaders of the returns. Zerubbabel was a prince of the tribe of Judah, of the house of David. Ezra was a priest of the tribe of Levi, of the house of Aaron. Nehemiah was the son of Hachaliah, of a tribe unknown to us.

The king is introduced:_____

The king's part is identified:_____

Ezra is introduced (cf. also v. 11):_____

_____

_____

Ezra's part is identified:_____

_____

_____

The Lord's part is recognized:_____

_____

_____

Facts of the journey:_____

_____

_____

How did Ezra take the initiative to make this journey a reality? _____

_____

On the phrase "prepared his heart" (v. 10), compare these verses: II Chronicles 12:14; 19:3; 30:19.

Now read the letter of the king to Ezra (7:11-26). What traits of Artaxerxes show here?_____

_____

Make a study of his references to God. Does he give any indication that he claimed God to be *his* God?_____

_____

2. THE PSALM (7:27-28). List the things for which Ezra was grateful to God. What do you learn about Ezra just from these two verses?_____

_____

_____

3. THE PEOPLE (8:1-14). Compare 2:3-15 and note that the two lists are virtually the same, and yet they refer to two different journeys eighty years apart. The explanation is that the names recorded are not those of individuals as such, but are family names. Add up the numbers recorded here to learn how many heads of families (8:3-14) accompanied Ezra (8:2 records heads of priestly houses).

4. THE PILGRIMAGE (8:15-32). Study this passage as a segment of four paragraphs, with divisions as shown below. (Mark these divisions in your Bible before reading the text.) As you read each paragraph, record your main observations below. Include in your observations the theme of each paragraph.

8:15-20	Then I sent
8:21-23	Then I proclaimed
8:24-30	Then I separated
8:31	Then we departed
8:32	And we came to Jerusalem

Read 8:15-20. How do verses 16-20 relate to the situation of verse 15: "I viewed . . . and found there none of the sons of Levi"?_____

_____

Compare this dearth of Levites with that of 2:36-42 (341

compared with 4,289 priests). What are some of the causes today for the dearth of Christian workers?_____

_____

_____

Read 8:21-23. What is the basic spirit underlying the true observance of fasting? (Read Judges 20:26; I Sam. 7:6; II Chron. 20:3.)_____

_____

What was Ezra's problem according to verse 22?_____

How do you account for the fact that Nehemiah didn't consider it wrong to have an escort (Neh. 2:9)?_____

Read 8:24-30. What spiritual truths are taught by verses 28 and 29a?_____

_____

Read 8:31-32. Compare 8:31 and 7:8 to determine the duration of the journey. Estimating the journey to be nine hundred miles long, calculate how many miles the Jews averaged each day. What was one obstacle which was overcome according to verse 31?_____

Observe how simply the fact of arrival in Jerusalem is reported: "And we came to Jerusalem" (8:32).

B. The Work (8:33—10:44).

The building of the temple had been completed during Zerubbabel's governorship (6:14), so Ezra did not have this responsibility when he arrived in Jerusalem. Yet his work centered about the temple. Read 7:18-20, 27 to recall what one of his tasks was, of a physical nature. Also read 7:10 again and note the spiritual ministry which Ezra intended to engage in during his stay in Jerusalem. Surely everything he accomplished is not recorded in the book of Ezra. That which is recorded shows how effectively Ezra

① **CONFESSION**
of Sin
in General

5

O my God, I am ashamed

② **ACKNOWLEDGMENT**
of God's Mercy
in the
Past

8

③ **CONFESSION**
of
Specific Sins

10

——— grace
——— remnant
———
———
———
. . . .

④ **ACKNOWLEDGMENT**
of Desert of
Destruction
in the Present

15

O Lord God . . . thou art righteous

was used of God to minister to the Jews in Palestine. (Note: See Chart J to review the outline of the passage you are about to study.)

1. THE PROGRAM (8:33-36). In these verses are recorded the two projects which were given first attention when Ezra's group arrived in Jerusalem. What were they?

8:33-34—

8:35—

For the temple-beautification project, the Jews had the assistance of the king's presidents and governors on the western side of the Euphrates River, who "helped the people in connection with the house of God" (8:36b). The program lasted for about four months (cf. 9:1a and 10:9).

2. THE PROBLEM (9:1-4). Read Exodus 34:16 and Deuteronomy 7:1-3 for the law which God had given His people and which they were now violating. The guilty ones were not only of Ezra's group of returnees, but also of the Jews already settled in the land. The problem did not originate

overnight. Why was Ezra's grief so intense?_____

_____

3. THE PRAYER (9:5-15). This is one of the Scriptures' strongest examples of prayer of contrition and confession. It surely deserves one's close scrutiny. As you study the prayer, record your observations on the analytical Chart K. The outlines already shown on the chart are starters for you, to suggest further studies. Observe how the first and third paragraphs are similar, and the second and fourth. Observe also how the prayer opens and closes.

Study carefully the various words of the second paragraph which represent God's help (e.g., grace, remnant). Record these on the chart. (For light on the meaning of "give us a nail in his holy place," see Isa. 22:23-25.)

Does Ezra ask for God's mercy in this prayer? What

may be learned from this?_____

_____

Had Israel learned from experience that man can limit the

application of God's long-suffering (e.g., in 722 B.C. and 586 B.C.)?

4. PENITENCE (10:1-4). Ezra's example of contrition was contagious, as these verses indicate. Someone other than Ezra suggested a way of deliverance (vv. 2-4). Could this have been Ezra's strategy of silence concerning hope—to cause the people *themselves* to recognize that they had come to the end of the line, and that they *must* cry out for mercy? Make a study of these important phrases in this paragraph:

"We have trespassed *against our God*."

"Yet now there is hope."

"Let us make a covenant *with our God*."

"Be of good courage, and do it."

5. PROPITIATION (10:5-17). The story of Ezra ends by showing how the sin of mixed marriages was dealt with, and how peace with God was thereby restored. (Recall the words "hope" and "covenant" of 10:2-3.)

The price of restoration was high. This is perhaps the main truth of these closing verses of Ezra. Observe the following in your study:

    a.   firm authority of God's spokesman (10:5)

    b.   deep remorse (10:6)

    c.   thorough investigation (10:7-8, 14)

    d.   no one excused from examination (10:8)

    e.   sense of fear (10:9, 14)

    f.   tragic consequences involved in the solution (10:44)

    g.   way to restoration (the word "propitiation" in our outline means atonement, or restored fellowship by sacrifice): confession of sin (10:11*a*), offering for sin (10:19), dissolution of marriage (10:11*b*)

Observe also that the physical setting of these days was as trying as the spiritual, for the people were standing in the open plazas in heavy rains so typical of cold, wet Decembers of the region (cf. 10:9, 13).

Derive some practical lessons from this passage, and list them here:_____

_____

_____

_____

_____

6. APPENDIX (10:18-44). Concerning the listed names of the guilty parties, observe that some priests, Levites and singers were involved. What is one practical purpose of Scripture in recording such lists?_____

_____

_____

What is the tragedy alluded to in verse 44?_____

_____

III. COMMENTS.

The Bible was not intended to be a complete chronicle of all the experiences of God's people through all the centuries. That which the Holy Spirit wanted recorded, however, found its place in the Holy Scriptures, as He inspired the authors to compose their writings. The book of Ezra skips over eighty years between chapters 6 and 7; and that which it does record about the ministry of Ezra includes only certain aspects, sufficient to fulfill the book's purpose.

In chapters 7—10 we learn again, as we did in chapter 1, how God sometimes uses unbelieving rulers to accomplish His divine purposes.

It is in these chapters also that we are introduced to the man Ezra. And what a man of God he was! He knew that if he was to be a successful minister of God's people, he first had to be in right relation to God. He "prepared his heart" to know what God's Word said and then to *live* that Word, so that he could teach his fellowmen this same Word (7:10).

"It seems that Ezra held a position at the Persian court corresponding to that of Secretary of State for Jewish affairs."‡ Ezra knew that if he was to secure permission from the king to lead a group of Jews back to Jerusalem, he must have the king's continued favor. We can be sure that Ezra was not an obnoxious, untactful, self-righteous Jew demanding the king's services. No king, with his supreme court ("seven counselors," 7:14), would ever send that kind of servant on such a coveted mission.

‡ *The Wycliffe Bible Commentary*, p. 430.

The four-month journey from Babylon to Jerusalem, following the route of the Fertile Crescent north of the Arabian desert, was about nine hundred miles. One can imagine the hardships attending such a mass migration of almost two thousand people, averaging seven miles a day. And yet not much is recorded in Ezra about those details.§ One item stands out because of its inclusion: the fasting and prayer for divine deliverance from evil bands of plunderers along the way (8:21-23).

Chapters 9 and 10 record much about the sin of the mixed marriages and Ezra's disposition of the problem. Although no word from God is recorded in these chapters —either in giving directions, or showing acceptance of the people's confessions and offerings—the absence of anything negative is a sound indicator of His approval of the disposition. God was not silent; His hand was upon Ezra (7:6, 28). And when this servant spoke concerning God's work he spoke *in behalf of God.* As a believing Jew he spoke to God for his brethren (9:6-15); and as a minister of God he spoke to his brethren for God (10:5, 10-11).

IV. CONCLUSION.

The book of Ezra opens on the bright note of a king's decree allowing the Jews to return to their homeland (1:1). It closes on the sad note of children made orphans when the marriage of their parents was dissolved (10:44). No book of the Bible contradicts the tragic fact of sin and its consequences. The evangel ("good news") of the Bible shines forth in all its glory when it speaks to this point. Such an evangel does not lead to despair, but points to heaven, from whence cometh the only help for the soul. Christ came from heaven to earth to die for our sins. He returned to heaven to wait until the day the number of His bride, the church, is complete. On that day He shall come again to receive His bride. What a glorious hope!

"Look up . . . for your redemption draweth nigh" (Luke 21:28).

§ There is a similar relative silence in the book of Numbers about many of the physical problems of the wilderness journey.

LESSON 6

BOOK OF NEHEMIAH
Background and Survey of Nehemiah

THE LAST OF OLD TESTAMENT HISTORY IS

RECORDED IN NEHEMIAH,* WHICH FOLLOWS

EZRA, WITH ABOUT TWELVE YEARS' INTERVAL.

Nehemiah is an invigorating and challenging book, showing what God can do through a remnant of believers who rise to God's call through His servant to restore a vital, worshipful relationship with Him. John C. Whitcomb makes this appraisal of the book:

> It must be said . . . that no portion of the Old Testament provides us with a greater incentive to dedicated, discerning zeal for the work of God than the Book of Nehemiah. The example of Nehemiah's passion for the truth of God's Word, whatever the cost or consequences, is an example sorely needed in the present hour.†

Problems, pains, prayer and perseverance are some of the ingredients of the "success" story of Nehemiah. If we look for inspiration as we study this wonderful book, we will surely experience it.

I. BACKGROUND.

A. Title of Book and Place in the Canon.

The book of Nehemiah is named after its main character and its opening words (1:1*a*). In all Old Testament canonical lists it has been classified as a historical book. Both Hebrew and Greek Bibles of the earliest centuries treated Ezra and Nehemiah as one book. The two-book classification of our English Bibles may be traced back to the Latin Vulgate Bibles.

---

* The events of Esther transpired just before Nehemiah, and in the middle of Ezra.
† *The Wycliffe Bible Commentary*, p. 435.

B. Date and Authorship.

Authorship of the book may be attributed to Nehemiah, who probably wrote most of it around 420 B.C. Some parts of the book contain his memoirs (1:1—7:5; 11:1-2; 12:27-43; 13:4-31). The list of Jewish families given in 7:5-73 was from a document already existing (the list is practically identical with that of Ezra 2:1-70). The third-person references to Nehemiah in 8:9; 10:1; 12:26, 47, do not contradict his authorship when the context is recognized.‡

C. The Man Nehemiah.

Nehemiah was born of Jewish parents in exile, and was given the name Nehem—Yah, meaning "the comfort of Jehovah." We may gather from this that Nehemiah's home was a godly one. At a young age he was appointed to the very responsible office of being cupbearer to King Artaxerxes. This was the contact which God used later in the granting of imperial permission for the return to Jerusalem of the third contingent of exiles, namely, Nehemiah and his project crew.

Nehemiah was truly a man of God, filled with the Spirit. He had a sensitive ear to God's voice concerning even the details of the work he was doing (2:12; 7:5). Prayer was a natural and essential part of his life. He knew what work was, and he worked and inspired others to do so. When opposition arose from the enemy, he stood strong and tall. He was alert also to the subversive plots of false brethren within the Jewish commonwealth. And when some of his own people became discouraged, he turned their eyes to the help of God, and found a ready response. Leader, worker, soldier, servant of God—this was Nehemiah.

D. Historical Background.§

There is a period of twelve years after the book of Ezra closes (457 B.C.) before the book of Nehemiah begins its story (cf. Ezra 7:8; 10:16-17 and Neh. 1:1; 2:1). Then Nehemiah records events of the next twenty years (445-425 B.C.).

Refer to Chart D and note the following:

---

‡ See *ibid.*, p. 435, for an explanation of this.
§ You may want to review Lesson 1, which covers the large historical background of all three books, Ezra, Nehemiah and Esther.

1. Artaxerxes I was king of Persia‖ when Nehemiah ministered.
2. 458 B.C.—Second return of Jews to Jerusalem, led by Ezra.
3. 446 B.C.—The enemies force the Jews to cease building the walls, and virtually destroy the parts already built (Ezra 4:23). News of this reaches Nehemiah (Neh. 1:3).
4. 445 B.C.—Nehemiah leads a small group of exiles to Jerusalem to organize the Jews already there to rebuild the walls. Nehemiah is appointed by Artaxerxes to be governor of Judah (a province of Persia at this time).
5. 444 B.C.—The walls project is completed (Neh. 6:15).
6. 433 B.C.—Nehemiah goes to Babylon on official business (cf. 2:6 and 13:6). The date 433 B.C. is derived from Nehemiah 5:14.
7. 420 B.C.—Nehemiah returns from Babylon (Neh. 13:7).

It must have been a heartwarming experience for Ezra when he learned that such a zealous believer as Nehemiah had arrived in Jerusalem with a new contingent of Jewish exiles.

While Nehemiah served as governor of Judah, Ezra was still ministering to the spiritual needs of the Jews there. (Ezra plays an important part in chaps. 8 and 12 of Nehemiah.)

Nehemiah also counted on the spiritual services of the Prophet Malachi during those last years of Old Testament history. Many of the evils denounced in the book of Malachi are part of the historical record of the book of Nehemiah.

E. Purposes.

In general, the book of Nehemiah seeks to show how God favored His people, so recently exiled, by strengthening their roots in the homeland of Judah in the face of all kinds of opposition.

Specifically, the book shows how the broken-down walls of Jerusalem and the failing faith of the Jews were restored, through (1) the competent leadership of Nehemiah, a man of prayer and faith; and (2) through a host of Jew-

‖ Persia at this time included the vast territory from India to Ethiopia, Judah being one of its provinces.

ish brethren who responded to the divine challenge to rise and build.

II. SURVEY.

For your survey of Nehemiah follow the general procedure outlined for the survey of Ezra in Lesson 2. Further suggestions are given below. Be sure to have pencil in hand as you read, marking your Bible for later reference.

A. First Reading.

Scan through the book, observing such things as organization of the book, and the prevailing atmosphere.

1. ORGANIZATION. Is there an introduction and conclusion to the book? _____

_____

Is the book mainly narrative? How much, if any, is autobiographical? _____

_____

Is there a progression? _____

A turning point? _____
Observe the places in the book where *lists* appear. These are of various kinds. Record the kinds and the references here:

LISTS	REFERENCES

2. ATMOSPHERE. What is the tone of the book in general? Reread the first few verses of each chapter and observe the *intensity* of the tone involved. Record phrases from the verses indicating this. (An example is given.)

1:4 "I . . . wept . . . mourned"   6:1
2:1   8:1
4:1   9:1
5:1   13:1

Observe also the simplicity in which the action is described. There are no embellishments of a litterateur attempting to give color to the drama. The intensity of the action remains even in the simplicity of the reporting. One writer has remarked, "We see throughout the writing of an honest, earnest man,—and through him the history closes with a sublime dignity."#

3. FIRST IMPRESSIONS. What are your first impressions of the book of Nehemiah? _____

_____

Does any passage of the book stand out prominently in your mind? If so, what? _____

_____

B. Second Reading.

For this slower reading there are other things to look for in Nehemiah. Record your observations on a survey chart similar to Chart L whenever possible.

1. Chapter titles. (Note the divisional points at 6:15; 7:73*b*; 12:27; and 12:44 shown on Chart L. Why are divisions made at these places?)
2. Key words and phrases. Always be on the lookout for these in Bible study.
3. Main characters. Among other things, note when Ezra appears in the story.
   Also, who are the most frequently mentioned enemies

John Peter Lange, *A Commentary on the Holy Scriptures, Nehemiah,* VII, 1.

Chart L

NEHEMIAH BUILDING FOR SECURITY

KEY VERSES: 2:17b; 6:3

KEY WORDS: build, remember, pray, wall, work, mercy, disobedience, thanksgiving

445 B.C. 444 415 B.C.

Prayer

Prayer

The Plans — Reconstruction — Resettlement — Revival — Redistribution — Rededication — Reform

Work Envisioned | Work Planned | Work Begun | Work Threatened from without—within—without | Work Finished | the law | the dependency | the will | the distribution | the dedication | the purging

Consecration | Revival | Consolidation

1 | 2 | 3 | 4 | 5 | 6:15 | 7:1 | 7:73b | 9:1 | 10:1 | 11:1 | 12:27 | 12:44 | 13:31

Building for Physical Security

Building for Spiritual Security

W O R K — builders

W O R S H I P — dwellers

Key: wall

Key: law

Leadership by a Man

Revival of a Nation

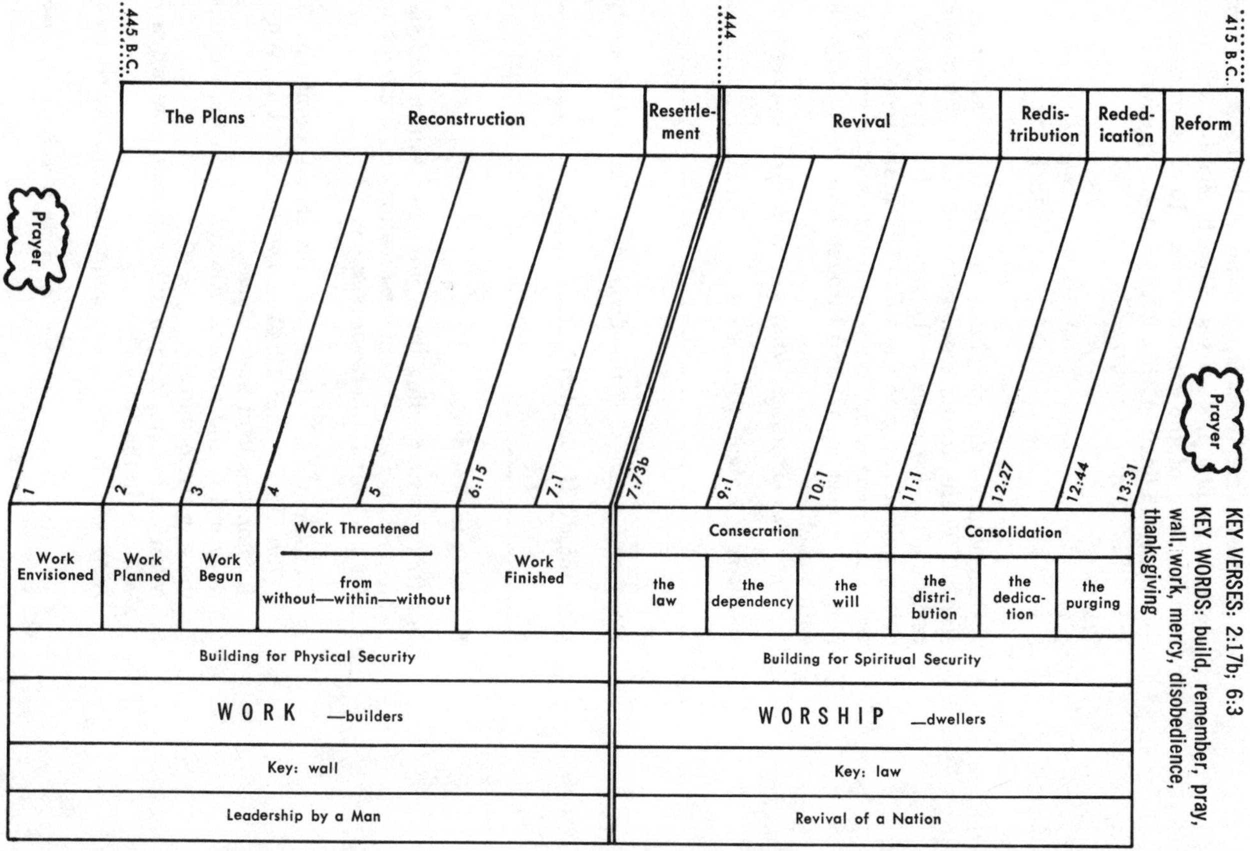

of Nehemiah? _____

_____

_____

4. What is the key event of the story? _____

_____

How is the book organized around this event? _____

_____

Try making some outlines of the book's story.
5. Theme of the book.
6. A key verse.
7. A title for the book.

C. A Survey Chart of Nehemiah.

Chart L shows how the book of Nehemiah may be graphically outlined. Compare the chart with your own work thus far, and then follow these study suggestions:
1. Make a note of the prayers of Nehemiah in the first and last chapters of the book.
2. Where is recorded the first operation of the building project? _____

What verse records the completion of the walls?_____

_____

How long did the project last?_____
3. Observe that 7:73b marks a turning point on Chart L. Some Bible students locate the main division at 7:1, which would make the passage 7:1-73a the opening of the second half of the book. Because of the nonnarrative nature of most of this passage, it may be considered either as the close of the first half or the opening of the second half of the book. The reason for this manual's including 7:1-73a in the first half of the book is that it relates more the aspect of *physical* security (cf. 7:1-4), whereas at 7:73b the narrative begins to focus on building for *spiritual* security (cf. 8:1).
4. The structure of the book of Nehemiah is very simple: two equal main parts, with each chapter adding a new point to the chapters preceding it.

5. Make a mental note of the key words cited on the chart. Also, read in your Bible the key verses and other verses shown.

6. The title used for Nehemiah is "Building for Security." What outline on the chart develops this title?

SUMMARY

The historians Ezra and Nehemiah have recorded for us practically all that is known of Jewish history during the restoration period from 538 to 425 B.C. Nehemiah's contribution was the firsthand account of the part he played especially in the rebuilding of Jerusalem's walls, a project not accomplished during the years covered by the book of Ezra.

It all began for Nehemiah while he was serving as cupbearer in the palace of Artaxerxes, King of Persia. When Nehemiah received news of the affliction and reproach of the Jewish remnant in Judah and the most recent desolation of Jerusalem's walls and gates, his heart burned with a sense of urgency that something must be done. Happily for Israel there were such men who still had faith in Jehovah as the Fulfiller, not the forgetter, of His covenant. These could not believe that there was no hope of revival and restoration for Israel as long as God had not broken His promises. How God stirred Nehemiah to lead his fellowmen in rebuilding what had been broken down—the city's walls, but more important the city's faith—is told in the book of Nehemiah.

The Building Project Is Born

WHEN KING ARTAXERXES SANCTIONED THE

DISRUPTION OF REBUILDING JERUSALEM'S

WALLS, NEHEMIAH WAS TOLD THE NEWS.

One of his brothers who lived in Jerusalem at the time made the long trip to Shushan to tell Nehemiah what had happened.* His report—brief and sad—is recorded in the first paragraph of the book of Nehemiah (1:1-3). The remainder of the book is the sequel to this report.

I. ANALYSIS.

For this segment (1:1—2:20) mark these paragraph divisions in your Bible: 1:1; 1:4; 2:1; 2:9; 2:17. Read the segment once or twice with these divisions in mind, making notations in your Bible of observations as you proceed with your study. The analytical Chart M may be used as a work sheet to record observations, including outlines. Study the outlines shown on Chart M after you have made a fairly thorough study of the passage yourself. The study suggestions given below will start you on paths of investigation.

1. Read 1:1-3. What were the two concerns of Nehemiah, and what were the two answers?_____

_____

What conditions may the phrase "great affliction" have described? _____

_____

What is meant by "reproach"? Compare this paragraph with 2:17-18. _____
2. Analyze carefully the second paragraph (1:4-11). This is a model prayer.

* The work was disrupted in 446 B.C.; Nehemiah heard the news in 445 B.C.

THE BUILDING PROJECT IS BORN
NEHEMIAH 1:1—2:20

(1) THE NEED	1:1	The wall . . . is broken down	The Situation Reported (secondhand)	
(2) A PRAYER FOR HELP Confession Claim Plea	4 1:11	I beseech thee (v. 5) I beseech thee (v. 8) I beseech thee (v. 11)	Prayer	the Help of God
(3) AN ANSWER TO THE PRAYER	2:1		Answer	the Help of a King
(4) THE NEED CONFIRMED	9		The Situation Viewed (firsthand)	
(5) WORKERS RECRUITED	17 Let us rise up and build 20		Rising To Build	the Help of the People

When you finish studying the prayer, list the many lessons on prayer which are taught here._____

_____

_____

_____

Observe on Chart M how the prayer is of three parts. Mark these in your Bible. What attributes of God does Nehemiah recognize in the prayer?_____

_____

_____

What is the *general* plea of verse 6?_____

_____

What is the *specific* plea of verse 11?_____

Are details given in this latter plea? Why did Nehemiah insert the last short sentence of the chapter immediately after the close of the prayer?_____

Why is confession of sin so important in prayer? (Compare the model prayer taught by Jesus in Luke 11:2-4.)

3. Read 2:1-8. Observe from verse 1 that the confident prayer of 1:5-11 did not dispel the sadness which was first recorded in 1:4. How do you account for this? (Cf. 2:3.)

What spiritual lesson is suggested by the *location* of the sentence "So I prayed to the God of heaven" (that is, the location between the question of 2:4a and the first phrase of 2:5a)?_____

What different favors did Nehemiah ask of the king?

_____

_____

Was this presumptious or demanding on the part of Nehemiah? Answer this in the light of the last sentence of 2:8.

_____

4. Read 2:9-16. What are some key phrases in this paragraph? _____

_____

Apparently no large contingent of Jews accompanied Nehemiah on this journey (cf. v. 9). The leaders mentioned in verse 16 are those who were already living in Jerusalem. The "rest that did the work" (v. 16) were probably those who had worked on the walls now destroyed. What was Nehemiah's purpose in making a secret survey of the walls before his speech of 2:17-20 to the leaders of the Jews in

Jerusalem? _____

_____

5. Read 2:17-20. At this point Nehemiah told the Jews about his assurance of God's help, and the sponsorship of King Artaxerxes. What was the people's immediate response? _____

Study carefully verse 20. What would God do for the

Israelites? _____

What would the Israelites do?_____

Apply this to Christian work today.

What spiritual lessons may be learned from the references to opposition in 2:10 and 2:19-20?_____

_____

_____

II. COMMENTS.

1. To read Nehemiah's prayer on the opening page of his book is to catch something of the tone of the book. For indeed, prayer is prominent throughout the narrative. Make a comparative study of these references to prayer: 1:4-11; 2:4; 4:4-5, 9; 5:19; 6:9, 14; 13:14, 22, 29, 31.

2. In the month Chisleu (Nov.-Dec.), Nehemiah received the distressing report from his brother, and began to weep, fast and pray (1:1). Four months later in the month Nisan (Mar.-Apr.), he was still mourning the state of Jerusalem (2:1). One important truth taught by this is that God doesn't always answer the prayer of faith *immediately*.

3. Artaxerxes gave Nehemiah permission to go to Jerusalem provided he returned to Shushan. The time originally set for the return (2:6) was probably changed later because, as it turned out, Nehemiah's stay in Jerusalem lasted twelve years (cf. 1:1; 5:14; 13:6).

4. Artaxerxes' letters of 2:7-9 were probably the "commandment to restore and build Jerusalem" (Dan. 9:25) prophesied by Daniel a century earlier, dating the beginning of the prophetic seventy years (read Dan. 9:24-27).

III. CONCLUSION.

Twice in this passage Nehemiah testifies of the *good hand of his God upon him* (2:8, 18). The events of the story demonstrate this divine blessing in Nehemiah's dealings with the following people:

the king—who favored Nehemiah (2:5)

the Jews—who responded to Nehemiah's challenge (2:18)

the enemies—who failed to intimidate Nehemiah (2:20)

Nehemiah was an able leader, gifted in many ways to do the Lord's work. He was a great inspirer of his people to get them to work—"Come . . . let us build" (2:17). Perhaps his greatest quality was his faith that God would give all the help needed for the awesome project of reconstruction. He couldn't have voiced this faith more wonderfully than when he said, "The God of heaven, he will prosper us" (2:20).

Reconstruction of the Walls and Gates

THE FIRST TWO CHAPTERS OF NEHEMIAH

SET THE STAGE FOR THE MAIN NARRATIVE—

A REBUILDING PROGRAM IN JERUSALEM.

At 3:1 we have the first reference to the actual building: "And they builded the sheep gate." At 7:73a is the reference to the people settling down in their homes, the building program having been completed. The progression of the early chapters of Nehemiah is this:

chap. 1	chap. 2	chaps. 3—7
Prayer	Preparation	Performance

Before beginning to analyze the chapters of the present lessons, fix in your mind an overview of this section (Chart N).

NEHEMIAH 3:1—7:73a   **Chart N**

3:1	4:1	5:1	6:1	6:15	7:73a
WORK BEGINS	WORK CONTINUES despite opposition from			Work is Finished	
	without	within	without		

I. ANALYSIS.

A. Work Begins (3:1-32).

This chapter is mainly a list of the projects and the workers. The things repaired were the gates and the walls between the gates. As you read the chapter, underline the reference to each gate. (Don't overlook the water gate of v. 26.) Geographically, the gates are listed in a counterclockwise order, beginning with the sheep gate in the north. (Note that the circuit returns to the sheep gate in v. 32.)

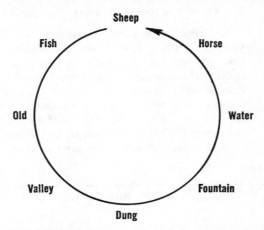

In applying this chapter (and the ones that follow) to the present day, follow this basic pattern of analogy:

BOOK OF NEHEMIAH	ILLUSTRATIVE OF
— the believing Jews — broken-down walls — rebuilding the walls	— Christians — aspects of the Christian life in need of restoration (e.g., prayer, worship, service) — revival and restoration

1. What practical truths are illustrated in these verbs:

"builded" (v. 1)_____

"sanctified" (v. 1)_____

"repaired" (v. 4, etc.)_____

"fortified" (v. 8)_____

2. "But their nobles put not their necks to the work of their Lord" (v. 5).* This is the only recorded exception at this time to an overall unity among the many workers.

* Some translate the word as "lord" (Nehemiah being meant).

3. No single gate or wall was more vital for defense than another. The completed wall would be only as strong as the weakest part. Apply this important truth to Christian service today.

B. Work Continues Despite Opposition (4:1—6:14).

1. OPPOSITION FROM WITHOUT (4:1-23; PARAGRAPH DIVISIONS AT VV. 1, 4, 6, 7, 16, 21). Various forms of opposition are reported in this chapter. Most of it came from outside the Jewish community. (Recall the opposition to Zerubbabel's project in Ezra 4:1-5.) But the building project continued without extended delay. Study the chapter to discover keys to victory in such trying circumstances. Follow the outline of the work sheet of Chart O, and record observations on the chart.

NEHEMIAH 4:1-23   Chart O

4:1-3 ①	**OPPOSITION of SCORN**
4:4-5	— prayer
4:6	— victory
4:7-15 ②	**OPPOSITION of CONSPIRACY** — prayer — more opposition — victory
4:16-20	**STRATEGY FORMULATED** watch and work
4:21-23	watch and work

a. Observe the repeated sequence of opposition, prayer, victory.

b. What do you learn about Nehemiah from this chapter?

_____

_____

c. What are the three voices of the opposition in verses 10-12? _____

_____

_____

(Read v. 12*b* thus, "They said unto us ten times from all places, Ye must return to us," ASV. The Jews living in the suburbs of Jerusalem were trying to recall the workmen on the walls to come and help them against the enemies' threats.)

d. What does verse 6 say was the reason for the continued progress of the building program?_____

e. Observe how verse 9 speaks of *prayer* and a *watch* (guard). Was such a watch a contradiction of faith? Explain. _____

What was the far-reaching effect of the watch (see v. 15)?

_____

f. Study verses 16-23. What strategy is emphasized in these verses?_____

_____

_____

What phrase or verse is your favorite here?_____

_____

2. OPPOSITION FROM WITHIN (5:1-19).† The reason for the Jews' complaint is given in verses 1-5.

a. Basically what was it? Note: For the phrase "We take up" (v. 2) read "Let us get" (ASV) or "We must be given" (Berkeley)._____

_____

b. The law forbade a Jew to lend money at interest to another Jew (Exodus 22:25; Deut. 23:19-20), and also to sell an Israelite as a slave (Lev. 25:42). Study verses 6-13 in view of these prohibitions. How do you explain the fact that the law is not mentioned in the chapter?_____

_____

c. What example for Christian living is to be seen in Nehemiah's actions of verses 14-19?_____

_____

3. OPPOSITION FROM WITHOUT (6:1-14). Scorn and military conspiracy were the two strategies of the enemy in chapter 4. Now the strategy was trickery with intent to murder Nehemiah. As you study these verses, observe especially Nehemiah's alertness to the enemies' devices, and his complete trust in God. Record your observations below.

The Enemy's Strategy	Nehemiah's Reply	Nehemiah's Trust
6:1-2a	6:2b-4	6:3 (implied)
6:5-7	6:8-9a	6:9b
6:10	6:11-13	6:12a, 14

† Some commentaries prefer to date the action of this chapter at a later time in the narrative, but there is sound basis for accepting the chronological location as it stands. Of course, vv. 14-19 form a parenthesis in the narrative, inserted as a commentary by Nehemiah concerning his relationship to the usury and tax problem *throughout* the entire twelve years of his governorship.

C. Work Is Finished (6:15—7:73a).

This section is of three parts: (1) building program completed (6:15-19); (2) Jerusalem guarded (7:1-4); and (3) families resettled (7:5-73a).

1. BUILDING PROGRAM COMPLETED (6:15-19). The first phrase of verse 15 and the last one of verse 16 are the key phrases here. What strikes you about the duration of the construction? _____

_____

_____

What is the main point of verse 16?_____

_____

The purpose of verses 17-19 is not to record new opposition that arose *after* the wall was finished but to expose another kind of opposition with which Nehemiah had to contend *during* the days of construction ("in those days"). How significant was it that the enemies of Israel concluded that God was the key to success in the building project?_____

_____

2. JERUSALEM GUARDED (7:1-4). The guard described here was Nehemiah's precaution against future attacks by the enemies (building for physical security). Verse 4 accentuates the need for a watch. Observe the spiritual traits of Hananiah (v. 2). What are some spiritual lessons taught in this paragraph?_____

_____

3. FAMILIES RESETTLED (7:5-73a). Now that the walls of Jerusalem had been rebuilt, Jews could safely dwell in the city. Up until now the Jews which returned with Zerubbabel had for the most part avoided living in this vulnerable spot. Hence the problem of 7:4. One of Nehemiah's purposes in registering the families according to the register of Zerubbabel's day was to establish the new generation's purity of genealogy. (Note: Except for vv.

70-72 the register of this chapter and that of Ezra 2:1-70 are identical.) The program of repopulating Jerusalem (see 11:1-2) would be based on this "reactivated" register. In the meantime the Jews continued to dwell in cities throughout the land (see 7:73).

How does 7:73*a* serve as a concluding verse for the first half of the book of Nehemiah?_____

_____

_____

II. COMMENTS.

Nehemiah was not a priest, scribe, prophet, rabbi, theologian or pastor. As a public official his vocation was secular, not religious. And yet, he clearly demonstrated in his service that spirituality is for the secular as well as the religious vocation.

The perseverance of Nehemiah in the face of persistent opposition by the enemy is a highlight of these chapters. Four times the enemy lured him to the village of Ono, and four times he resolutely refused. "Why should the work cease, whilst I leave it, and come down to you?" (6:3). David Livingstone voiced the same determination when people urged him to leave Africa and return to the homeland: "No, it must not, will not, cannot be. I must finish the work I started."

Satan is our adversary, and goes about "seeking whom he may devour" (I Peter 5:8). We may be sure that Satan will exert his utmost ability to keep us from the revival and renewal of heart which we seek. He rejoices over backslidden believers, and roars violently when he knows there has been repentance of heart. But the Word of God assures us that if we persistently resist the devil as we submit ourselves to God, the devil will flee from us (James 4:7). Satan cannot move God.

III. A SUMMARY EXERCISE FOR NEHEMIAH 1:1—7:73a.

The first half of the book of Nehemiah teaches valuable lessons on *service for God*. Think back over these chapters and list at least ten such lessons which you have seen in your study.

IV. A CONCLUDING THOUGHT.

The completion of the building project was a blow to the enemies of Israel. Nehemiah reports that they were much cast down, "for they perceived that this work was wrought of our God" (6:16). Such are the concluding words of the first half of Nehemiah (exclusive of the parenthesis of 6:17-19). Even enemies of God's children can be made to perceive the hand of God in the lives of His own. Are we giving God His rightful place in our lives as He works in and through us?

Revival

A MAJOR TURN IS MADE AS THE STORY

SHIFTS FROM THE PHYSICAL REBUILDING

TO BUILDING FOR SPIRITUAL SECURITY.

It is in chapter 8 that Ezra the scribe appears in the book of Nehemiah for the first time. Also, the autobiographical "I" of chapters 1—7 now becomes the biographical "Nehemiah" (8:9), to return to the "I" at 12:31. Review Chart L and observe other comparisons of the two main divisions of Nehemiah, such as

WORK	WORSHIP
Key: Wall	Key: Law

The three chapters of this lesson may prove to be the most spiritually fruitful ones of your entire study of Ezra-Nehemiah-Esther. The reading of God's Word is given no higher honor than in chapter 8; thanksgiving and penitence are blended together in sublime and startling proportions in the prayer of chapter 9; and the people's determination to prove the sincerity of that prayer by action is wonderfully exemplified in chapter 10.

The subject of *revival* is often discussed by Christians, but seldom experienced. Revival is the renewal of the believer's intimate relationship with God. The price of revival is high, but the way is simple. These three chapters present that way, in the correct order:

Chapter 8: the work of God's Word (exposure to, and understanding of the Word)

Chapter 9: The experience of genuine prayer (confession of sin, and worship of God)

Chapter 10: decision and action (in the spirit of sacrifice)

As you begin your study of these three chapters, be satisfied with your answers to the question Do I need revival, and if so, do I want revival?

Chart P shows a simple outline of the chapters of this lesson. As you study the passage you will probably want to make other comparisons.

NEHEMIAH 7:73b—10:39   Chart P

7:73b	9:1	10:1 10:39
Law Is Read	Confession Is Made	Oath Is Sealed
— gladness —	— fasting —	— submission —
R E V I V A L		

I. ANALYSIS.

A. The Law Is Read (7:73b—8:18; paragraph divisions at 7:73b; 8:9; 8:13).

Study this portion with this title in mind: "Fruits of the Word When It Is Read." The three paragraphs suggest three fruits:

1. UNDERSTANDING (7-73b—8:8). Visualize the setting and action of this emotion-packed occasion. Note the repeated word "all" in the paragraph. The date was the first day of the seventh month (8:2), one week after the wall had been finished (cf. 6:15). It was the beginning of the civil year, and also the Feast of Trumpets. The week-long Feast of Tabernacles (referred to in 8:14) was also observed in this month, beginning on the fifteenth day.*

Make a list of all the things Ezra did, and the people's responses. What is the prevailing atmosphere of this para-

graph? _____

Study especially the repeated word "understand" here. Observe from verses 7 and 8 that help was given the people

---

* The Day of Atonement fell on the tenth day of this same month, though this holy day is not mentioned in the narrative.

so that they could understand the Scripture. What kind of help may this have been?_____

_____

2. JOY (8:9-14). What reasons are given in this paragraph for the people's joy?†_____

_____

In what ways does the Bible fill your heart with gladness?

_____

_____

3. DISCOVERY (8:13-18). Read Leviticus 23:33-43, Numbers 29:12-40, and Deuteronomy 16:13-17 to see what it was that the Israelites "found written in the law" which they had not been observing. The feast of the seventh month, about which the people read, is called by different names: Feast of Tabernacles, Feast of Booths, or Feast of Ingathering. What did the booths symbolize?

_____

_____

Why was this feast such a joyous one?_____

_____

Has it been your experience that the more you read and study the Bible the more you discover truths you had not known before?

B. Confession Is Made (9:1-38).

In this chapter is recorded the longest prayer of the Bible. One of the best surveys of Old Testament history is given in the prayer. Study the chapter carefully, and record observations, outlines and applications on the work sheet

† Concerning national mourning, it may be noted that the Day of Atonement, which was about ten days away, was the only day of the year which God singled out for mourning and weeping of the kind referred to in 8:9.

of Chart Q. A simple threefold outline is suggested by the three prominent pronouns "thou," "they" and "we."

NEHEMIAH 9:1-38

THE PRAY-ERS	THE PRAYER		
1	God of Israel	Forefathers of Israel	Present Distress of Israel
	4 "Thou"	16 "They"	32 "We"
			38

C. Oath Is Sealed (10:1-39).

This chapter reveals that the Jews' repentance for sin was not only of contrition but also of a positive determination to *obey the Word of God*. This is the strength of the oath which was made and written by the people and sealed by their leaders. (Compare the last sentence of the prayer, 9:38, with 10:1-29a.)

Observe the *general* commitments of the oath in 10:29. Then note that the remainder of the chapter records *specific* resolutions made by the people. Identify these:

v. 30:

v. 31:

vv. 32-39: (The key phrase of this paragraph is "we will not forsake the house of our God," 10:39. Observe the repetitions of the phrase "house of our God.")

Can you make any application for present-day living from this chapter?_____

_____

_____

_____

II. COMMENTS.

1. "For everything there is an appointed season, and there is a proper time for every project under heaven . . . a time to weep, and a time to laugh . . ." (Eccles. 3:1-4, Berkeley). When Ezra read the Scriptures to the people, it was a time for joy, because (1) the project of the wall had just been completed, and (2) the time was the Feast of Trumpets, the beginning of the new civil year, with its appeal to the forward look (similar to our New Year's Day). It was a "solemn" day (cf. Lev. 23:24; Num. 29:1) and "holy" (Neh. 8:9-11), but a day of joy and gladness. On the Day of Atonement (the tenth day of this same month) the atmosphere was very different, being one of fasting and godly sorrow for sins which needed atonement.

2. "So they [Ezra and his assistants] read in the book in the law of God distinctly [ASV marg., "with an interpretation"], and gave the sense, and caused . . . [the people] to understand the reading" (Neh. 8:8). This may be a

reference to the use of Aramaic targums, which were expanded paraphrases of Scripture intended to throw light on the Word in the vernacular of the people.‡ F. F. Bruce says, "It seems reasonable to infer that as the Law was read aloud in Hebrew, an oral interpretation in Aramaic was also provided for those to whom Hebrew was no longer familiar."§ Whatever method was employed, interpretations and explanations were given to the people, so that they could "understand the reading." By so understanding, they would want to live their lives in obedience to God's Word.

III. SUMMARY.

Reading and understanding God's Word, confession of sin, and committing all of one's being to the Lord are the three main ingredients of Israel's revival recorded in these chapters. The people solemnly covenanted "to walk in God's law," which they were proud to claim as having come to them through "Moses the servant of God" (10:29). Among other things they said, "We will not forsake the house of our God" (10:39).

The passing of time would tell how faithfully they and their children would keep this covenant.

‡ At this time Aramaic was the everyday language of the Jews, most of whom had become alienated from pure Hebrew as a vernacular during the captivity years. Hence, when Scripture was read in Hebrew, many Jews had difficulty grasping the content.

§ F. F. Bruce, *The Books and the Parchments*, p. 53.

Consolidation

THE LAST CHAPTERS OF NEHEMIAH RECORD

IMPORTANT ASPECTS OF ISRAEL'S LIFE AS

THEY ENTER THE PHASE OF CONSOLIDATION.

Those aspects are: the nation's size and distribution; the nation's defense; and the nation's purity. The same subjects appeared earlier in the book, but in a slightly different context. Chart R gives a survey of this final section of Nehemiah. Mark the divisions in your Bible, with the outlines,* as a guide for your reading.

NEHEMIAH 11:1—13:31   Chart R

11:1	12:27	12:44 13:31
REGISTERED LISTS	OFFICIAL DEDICATION	NECESSARY REFORMS
— families —	— walls —	— laws —
The nation's size and distribution	The nation's defense	The nation's purity

* Some outlines extend the middle dedication section to include verses through 13:3, based on the phrase "on that day" of 13:1. It may be noted, however, that the same Hebrew word for that phrase is translated "at that time" in 12:44. Concerning this *The Wycliffe Bible Commentary* writes, "This phrase . . . refers not only to the dedication day, but possibly also to the entire subsequent administration of Nehemiah, which was characterized by reform movements" (p. 444). It is with this in mind that the outline of Chart R shows the section "Necessary Reforms" as beginning at 12:44. (Observe the various time references in this last section: "at that time," 12:44; "in the days of Nehemiah," 12:47; "on that day," 13:1; "before this," 13:4; "in all this time," 13:6; "in those days," 13:15, 23.)

I. ANALYSIS.

A. Registered Lists (11:1—12:26).

1. Read 11:1-2. Recall the problem of 7:4. Why had Jews hesitated about settling down in the city of Jerusalem?___

_____

How was the problem solved?_____

_____

Were the lots of verse 1 and the voluntary offers of verse 2 two different solutions?_____

_____

2. Mark this outline in your Bible for 11:3—12:26:
   a. people dwelling in Jerusalem (11:3-24)
   b. other towns where Jews dwelt (11:25-36)
   c. priests and Levites who returned with Zerubbabel (12:1-9)
   d. high priests, priests and Levites in later years (12:10-26)

Make a note of any phrases in the listings which suggest practical lessons, such as "the principal to begin the thanksgiving in prayer" (11:17).

B. Official Dedication (12:27-43).

1. As you read the passage, observe especially the atmosphere of the dedication services, and the main activities.
2. Observe the return of Nehemiah's "I" in verse 31. What was the reason for appointing two great companies

(12:31-43)? _____

_____

What group did Nehemiah join?_____

_____

Ezra? _____
What is the significance of the wives' and children's participation (12:43)?_____

_____

12:44-47

13:1-3

13:4-9

13:10-14
Remember me, O my God,

13:15-18

13:19-22
Remember me,

13:23-27

13:28-29
Remember them

13:30-31
Remember me

3. What are some spiritual lessons taught in this passage?

_____

_____

_____

_____

C. Necessary Reforms (12:44—13:31).

Use the work sheet of Chart S as a place to record your observations as you study these paragraphs.
1. Record the various reforms instituted. Concerning 13:4-9, who was Tobiah, and what part did he play in the

earlier chapters of the book?_____

_____

2. Record key words and phrases.
3. Make a comparative study of Nehemiah's prayers. Recall Nehemiah's prayer in the opening chapter of the book.
4. Note the reference to Nehemiah's extended leave in Babylon (13:6-7), which may have lasted for as many as eight years (433-425 B.C.). How intense was Nehemiah's

reaction for what he saw when he returned?_____

_____

Why is it so important for leaders and shepherds in God's work to be constantly on the watch for evils, and to

expose them?_____
5. Compare the question of 13:11 with the earlier vow of 10:39. What does this reveal about human nature?

_____

_____

6. Are the kinds of sins mentioned in these verses preva-

lent in the church today?_____
What valuable lessons can we learn from this passage?

_____

_____

_____

*   *   *

CONCLUDING REMARKS

We have come to the end of our study of the book of Nehemiah. The book has taught us much about God, and His work, and the servants through whom He has chosen to accomplish that work.

The Israelites were constantly in need of spiritual revival in Old Testament times. Ezra led them in one movement. Twelve years later when Nehemiah arrived there was another stirring, fanned by the preaching of Malachi, and repeated again when Nehemiah returned from Babylon the second time. Then, after Nehemiah and Malachi had passed away, came the "400 silent years" of Jewish history, lived by generations who were generally of stony hearts. We cannot measure the extension of Nehemiah's ministry into those "silent" years but, as one author has said, "we may believe that his influence ran down private channels in families and humble houses to the very time of the Messiah, making green lines of spiritual growth amid the arid desert of Judaism."†

What Christian living today should not covet the zeal of Nehemiah in the work of the Lord's vineyard? Here was "a man of strong convictions and of forceful character. . . . Whether dealing with friend or enemy he was always forthright and direct, often indeed to the point of bluntness and of what we today probably would call 'tactlessness.' Pervading every atom of his being was a flaming zeal for the Lord and for His work. . . . Oh, that God might raise up even a few in our own day, for once again the 'walls' are crumbling and the foe is attacking."‡

---

† John Peter Lange, *A Commentary on the Holy Scriptures, Nehemiah*, VII, 58.

‡ G. Coleman Luck, *Ezra-Nehemiah*, p. 126.

BOOK OF ESTHER
Background and Survey of Esther

NOW WE RETURN TO A TIME EARLIER THAN

NEHEMIAH, FOR ESTHER'S SETTING IS

DATED BETWEEN CHAPTERS 6 AND 7 OF EZRA.

The Old Testament history of Israel closes with the last chapter of Nehemiah (c. 425 B.C.). Were it not for the events of the book of Esther, however, there may not have been a story for Nehemiah to record. Esther was included in the biblical account to show how God's chosen people were spared extermination during their exilic years. It is a story that should inspire Christians today to an increased trust in God who sovereignly controls world history and preserves His own children.

I. BACKGROUND.

A. Title.
The title "Esther" is assigned to this book because Esther is its main character. Jews call the book Megilloth Esther (Esther Roll) because it is one of the five rolls assigned for reading at Jewish holidays.*

B. Authorship and Date.

Authorship of the book is unknown. The author was probably a Jew living in Persia during the latter half of the fifth century B.C. when the action of the book took place. Some have suggested Ezra or Nehemiah as possible authors, on the basis of similarity of writing style.

---

* Esther is read at the Feast of Purim (Mar. 14-15).

C. Place in the Canon.

The book of Esther is listed last in the historical books of the English Bible, and eighth in the Writings (Kethubhim) section of the Hebrew Bible. Though its canonicity has been challenged by some, it has remained firmly in the canon.† The Jews have always accepted the book as canonical.

D. The Lady Esther.

Esther was a Jewish orphan maiden who lived in Shushan, Persia's principal capital city. She was reared by a cousin, Mordecai, who was an official in the king's palace (2:15). King Xerxes (Ahasuerus‡) chose Esther to be the new queen of Persia after he had divorced his wife. Through Esther's influence Jews living in Persia were spared extermination.

The name Esther ('ester) may have been derived from the Persian word for "star" (sitareh). Esther's Hebrew name was Hadassah (2:7), which means "myrtle."

It is interesting to note that only one other book in the Bible is named after a woman: Ruth. One writer has made this comparison: "Ruth was a Gentile woman who married a Jew. Esther was a Jewish woman who married a Gentile."§

The story of Esther reveals a woman of very commendable character. Among her traits were genuine piety, faith, courage, patriotism, compassion, maturity and natural charm. Your study of the book of Esther will show how such a woman was used of God in the interests of His chosen people, the Jews.

E. Historical Background.

History always originates in *places*, so it is helpful first to visualize the geography of the book of Esther. Refer to the map on Chart B and observe the location of Shushan

---

† Some Bibles (e.g., Catholic) add "Additions to Esther" (10:4—16:24) to the canonical book, intended mainly to compensate for the absence of the name of God. The fact that no portion of the book of Esther has yet been discovered in the Qumran area (place of the Dead Sea Scrolls discoveries) indicates that the Essenes of Qumran probably rejected the canonicity of Esther.

‡ The term Ahasuerus may have been a Persian title for "king," rather than a name, similar to the title "pharaoh." Hence the Berkeley Version translates Esther 1:1 thus: "In the days of Ahasuerus. . . ." In any case, the king referred to as Ahasuerus was Xerxes.

§ John Phillips, *Exploring the Scriptures*, p. 91.

(Greek Susa) in Persia,‖ where Esther lived and served as queen. (This is the same city where Daniel had received a vision from God about eighty years earlier, Dan. 8:2.) Some have estimated that between two and three million Jews were living in Persia and Babylon during the time of the book of Esther. Read Esther 1:1 and note the extensive domain of Xerxes, king of Persia: 127 provinces from India to Ethiopia.

The story of Esther took place between the first return of exiles under Zerubbabel (536 B.C.) and the second return under Ezra (458 B.C.). Chart T shows the major points of this historical setting.

Observe the following:

1. The events of this book cover a period of ten years (483-473 B.C.). If one would see in 10:1 an indirect reference to the death of King Xerxes (d. 464 B.C.), then it could be said that the book covers a span of about twenty years.

2. Xerxes was the king of Persia during all of this period.

3. All of the book is dated between chapters 6 and 7 of Ezra.

4. The book opens with a feast (Xerxes) and closes with a feast (Purim). The former was to honor the king and his empire; the latter was to commemorate the Jews' deliverance.

It is interesting to observe that around the time of the book of Esther three great world battles were fought (Salamis, Thermopylae and Marathon), and two great world leaders died (Confucius and Buddha).

F. Purpose of the Book.
The major purpose of the book of Esther is to show how a host of Jews living in exile were saved from being exterminated by the hand of a Gentile monarch. Though no name of God appears in the book, the divine Providence pervades the narrative.# It is the same Providence that preserved the nation of Israel in the oppressions of Pharaoh, and through such devastating judgments as those of the wilderness journeys, the Assyrian and Babylonian

‖ The modern name for Persia is Iran.
Matthew Henry writes, "If the name of God is not here, His finger is."

Chart T

HISTORICAL SETTING OF ESTHER

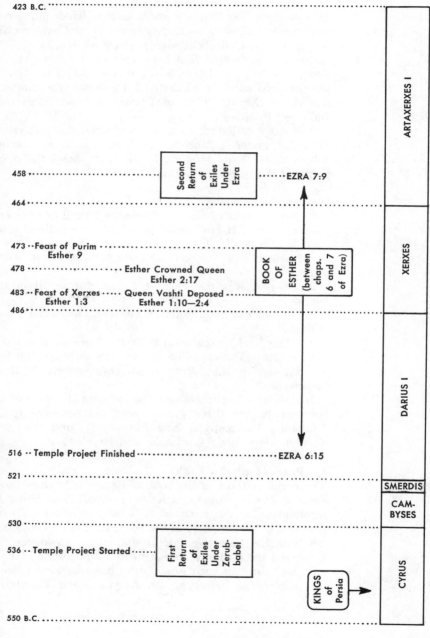

423 B.C.

ARTAXERXES I

458 — Second Return of Exiles Under Ezra — EZRA 7:9

464

473 — Feast of Purim — Esther 9

478 — Esther Crowned Queen — Esther 2:17

483 — Feast of Xerxes — Queen Vashti Deposed — Esther 1:3 — Esther 1:10—2:4

486

BOOK OF ESTHER (between chaps. 6 and 7 of Ezra)

XERXES

DARIUS I

516 — Temple Project Finished — EZRA 6:15

521

SMERDIS

CAM-BYSES

530

536 — Temple Project Started — First Return of Exiles Under Zerubbabel

KINGS of Persia →

CYRUS

550 B.C.

invasions, the destruction of Jerusalem in A.D. 70, and Hitler's mass slaughters.

Other related truths taught by the book will be seen as you proceed in your study of the text.

G. Special Points.

Two special points about the book of Esther will be cited here.

1. A KEY WORD OF THE BOOK IS "JEW." The singular form appears eight times; the plural form, forty-three times. The term Jew is derived from the word Judah. Since most of the returning exiles were of the tribe of Judah, the title Jew was applied to them, and extended in later years to all Hebrew people.

2. A NOTABLE EXCLUSION IS ANY NAME OF GOD. Also, there are no explicit references to prayer, worship, the law, Jerusalem or the temple. Yet Esther stands firmly in the canon of Scripture as an inspired book of God.** One explanation of the exclusion is that because these Jews living in Esther's time had disassociated themselves from the theocratic institution when they refused King Cyrus' permission to return to Palestine (recorded in the early chapters of Ezra), God's name was not at this time linked with them as such, though continued providence and future covenant dealings with the nation were not thereby annulled.

II. SURVEY.

For your survey study of the book of Esther, follow the procedures shown earlier in this manual. Scan through the book once or twice, to see the highlights of the narrative.

Four people are the main characters of the book: King Ahasuerus, Esther, Mordecai and Haman. As you read each chapter, observe the part played by any of these characters, and record this on the survey Chart U. This will give you a good grasp of the multifaceted plot of this true story.

Study the outlines on Chart U, comparing them with your own observations made during the survey reading. Note also the title given the book, and the key verse and key words.

** Additions to Esther appear in some Bibles (e.g., Catholic versions), but these are Apocryphal additions.

ESTHER BOOK OF PROVIDENTIAL CARE

82

A KEY VERSE: 4:14b

KEY WORDS: Jew (51x), feast

Feast of God's Prince Mordecai (chap. 9)

Feast of the World's Prince Ahasuerus (chap. 1)

473 B.C.

Exaltation of a Jew

Deliverance of the Jews

Influence of a Jewess

474
479

Threat Against the Jews

480

Elevation of a Jewess

483 B.C.

Gentile Setting

Feasts of Ahasuerus

Feast of Purim

Feast of Esther ②

Feast of Esther ①

Honoring the New Queen

Honoring the Glorious Kingdom

10:1

9:17

8

7

6

5

4

3

2

1

The Jews Are Spared

The Jews Are Threatened

Exal-tation

Commem-oration

Deliverance

Plot

Setting

Observe the elevation of a Jewess, Esther, in chapter 2, and the exaltation of a Jew, Mordecai, in chapter 10.

What were the occasions for the feasts of the book?

_____

_____

_____

III. A CONCLUDING EXERCISE.

Keep in mind your overview of the book of Esther as you answer the following questions.

1. In what sense is Esther a book of providential care?

_____

_____

2. Name one important truth taught by the fact of God's deliverance of the Jews in Esther's day._____

_____

3. What is God's interest in the Jews today, and what is the reason for it?_____

_____

4. Derive a few spiritual lessons from the key verse 4:14b: "Who knoweth whether thou art come to the kingdom for such a time as this?" Keep this verse clearly in mind as you proceed with your chapter-by-chapter analysis of Esther in the next lessons.

The Jews Are Threatened

ESTHER 1—3 DESCRIBES THE SETTING,

INTRODUCES MAIN CHARACTERS, AND

UNFOLDS THE BEGINNINGS OF THE STORY.

As you study these chapters and the ones that follow, your aim should be more than learning the mere facts, important as such facts are. Try to discover what is behind the facts, and what spiritual truths are disclosed. You will especially want to learn about the sovereignty of God, including good things He efficiently wills, and evil things He permits. These are taught in the book even though, as we have already seen, the name of God does not appear in the text. Also, you will want to learn about the fortunes of the Jews, about whom the story of Esther revolves, during the exile years of 483-473 B.C.

I. HISTORICAL SETTING.

These few historical notes indicate the secular backdrop of the story of Esther in these chapters:

  1. The feast of chapter 1 is dated 483 B.C., when King Ahasuerus discussed plans with his staff concerning his forthcoming invasion of Greece.

  2. The Persians were defeated by the Greeks in the battles of Thermopylae and Salamis (481-479 B.C.). This campaign took place after chapter 1 and probably during the first part of chapter 2.*

  3. Esther was made queen (2:17-18) in 479 B.C.

  4. Chapter 3 may be dated 474 B.C. (see 3:7; 2:16).

II. ANALYSIS.

Read 1:1—3:15 once or twice to become acquainted with the narrative. Underline key words and phrases in your Bible as you read.

---

* See *The Wycliffe Bible Commentary*, p. 449.

Use the empty boxes of Chart V to record the main content of each part of the passage (each box represents either a paragraph or a group of paragraphs).

ESTHER 1:1—3:15

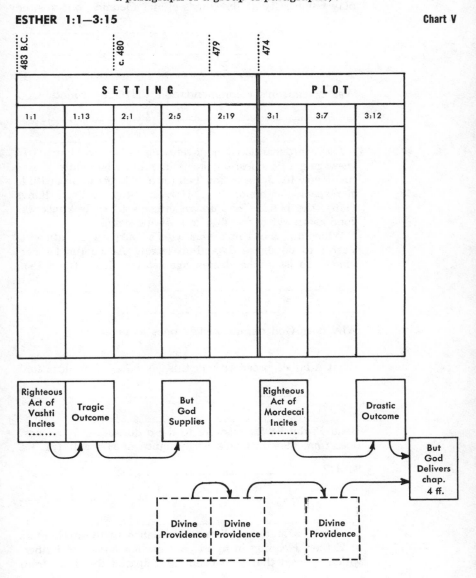

1. Make a study of righteous acts and evil acts in this passage. (Complete the outline of this subject which appears on Chart V.) Did Vashti do right in refusing to display her beauty at the king's affair? Defend your answer.

_____

_____

_____

Was Memucan's recommendation (1:16-20) sound?_____

_____

_____

Did Mordecai do right in refusing to bow to Haman? In answering this question, keep in mind that while it was customary for Jews to bow before their kings in an attitude of respect and honor (e.g., II Sam. 14:4; 18:28; I Kings 1:16), the bowing of Persian citizens to their kings was done as an act of worship to a divine being.

What do you think was God's purpose in allowing Vashti to be deposed, and in letting Ahasuerus be persuaded to issue the decree against the Jews (3:10-15)?

_____

_____

Why does God permit wicked ones to prosper?_____

What kind of prosperity is this, and for what duration?

_____

_____

Read Psalm 94 for answers to these questions. What part does *time* play in God's performance of His will (cf. Ps. 94:3)? _____

_____

_____

2. Make a study of divine providence in these chapters of Esther. Keeping in mind your earlier survey of Esther, which showed that God eventually spared the Jews from

being exterminated (chaps. 8—9), identify the events of chapters 1—3 which were providential causes and means of the eventual deliverance. Record your answers on Chart V, in the boxes provided. Look for other providential acts.

III. COMMENTS.

1. The book of Esther opens on a high note, from a secular standpoint, but quickly descends to the low. The movement is from palatial splendor, to the indulgences of revelry, to the expulsion of the queen. How true it is that not all is beautiful which appears beautiful. We as Christians need to remind ourselves that multitudes who outwardly appear satisfied with their lot are sinners condemned to eternal death, in desperate need of salvation.

2. The courage of Queen Vashti in refusing to surrender her modesty and noble womanhood to a husband sporting in drunken revelry must be highly commended. It is interesting to observe that the new queen chosen by Ahasuerus was even nobler than Vashti. The choice, of course, was of divine providence.

3. Mordecai's courageous refusal to bow to Haman reminds one of Daniel's stand regarding praying (Dan. 6:10). In these last days Christians can expect more and more that their religious convictions will be challenged by secular powers. A clear guideline for the Christian's answer in such a situation is Peter's firm statement "We ought to obey God rather than men" (Acts 5:29).

When Mordecai told why he was disobeying the king's commandment, he disclosed for the first time that he was a Jew, or Jehovah-worshiper. Haman knew then that to uproot this problem of opposition he must exterminate *all* Jews, not just one man (3:6). It was not difficult for him to convince his superior, the king, to fulfill his wishes (3:8-11). Such was a consequence of the homogeneous quality of Jewry in those days, a quality that has remained to the present day.

4. Little did Mordecai know that his saving the king's life (2:19-23) would effect his own deliverance in a few years. "Cast thy bread upon the waters: for thou shalt find it after many days. Give a portion to seven, and also to eight; for thou knowest not what evil shall be upon the earth" (Eccles. 11:1-2).

IV. CONCLUDING REMARKS.

The last phrase of chapter 3 is significant: "But the city Shushan was perplexed." Not only Jews but non-Jews reacted to this outrageous example of violent despotism. Sometimes the masses are wrong, but not always. Here was a situation where a king and his high minister were an erring minority with extensive authority. But all people—nations and individuals alike—must reckon with the highest Authority—God. The king's decree was issued and posted, but the King of kings would have the last word. This is the story of the next chapters of Esther.

Influence of a Jewess

THE VAST INFLUENCE OF WOMEN, AND

ESPECIALLY MOTHERS, UPON THE COURSE

OF THIS WORLD MUST BE ACKNOWLEDGED.

This is surely true of mothers because "the hand that rocks the cradle is the hand that rules the world." It is also true of women raised up of God from time to time for a special work in a particular situation. Such was the sovereignly determined lot of Queen Esther, who was in a position to appeal to the king to spare the Jews from the planned pogrom. Her foster-father Mordecai saw the hand of God in this when he exclaimed to her, "Who knoweth whether thou art come to the kingdom for such a time as this?!" (4:14).*

As of chapter 3, the extermination of all Jews in Xerxes' empire awaited merely the arrival of the day of slaughter, eleven months later, on the thirteenth of Adar (3:13). That date had been determined by lot ("Pur," see 3:7). The decree was distributed in letter form by couriers throughout the empire, ordering the authorities "to destroy, to kill, and to cause to perish, all Jews, both young and old, little children and women, in one day" (3:13). Why the king turned against Haman, instigator of the plot, is the subject of this lesson.

I. SURVEY OF THE PASSAGE.

You may want to make a survey reading of the four chapters before analyzing each chapter individually. Chart W gives a brief overview of the passage. Refer to it as you read the chapters.

* Mordecai's words quoted here are a good illustration of the combination question-exclamation, a modern innovation of punctuation called "interrabang."

89

4:1	5:1	6:1	7:1	7:10
Audience with the King Planned	King Favors Esther	King Honors Mordecai	King Hangs Haman	

Esther's First Banquet   Esther's Second Banquet

Grief of the Persecuted Ones (4:1-4) → Death of the Persecutor 7:8-10

II. ANALYSIS.

Topical Bible study is always an interesting method of study. Below are suggested some subjects for you to consider in your analysis of these chapters.

A. Grief of the Jews.

Who are the mourners of 4:1-4?_____

_____

Note the reference to fasting in 4:16. Do you think that prayer to God was involved here, even though it is not

specifically mentioned? (Cf. Joel 1:14.)_____

_____

_____

B. Religious Faith of Mordecai and Esther.

As you study these chapters and the ones of the next lesson, try to determine whether Mordecai and Esther personally put their trust in Jehovah God. We have already observed that no name of God is spoken by them in the book. Does this preclude the possibility that they were believers?

C. Providence of God.

Make this your key study in these chapters. Observe the following factors which were brought about providentially so that the Jews would not be slaughtered.

1.   The distant date of execution allowed for favorable events to take place in the meantime. What was the providence of God in 3:7?_____

_____

2.   The optimistic insight of Mordecai caused him to influence the queen to action (4:13-17). Study the context of Esther's statement "If I perish, I perish." Did she say this in a fatalistic mood, or was she brought to see the guiding hand of God, whatever was the outcome?_____

_____

_____

3.   Esther obtained favor in the king's sight (5:1-8). What if it had been otherwise?_____

_____

4.   Esther was led to delay her accusation against Haman by one day (5:8). This allowed for the events of chapter 6 to take place in the meantime (unanticipated by Esther, of course).

5.   The king had a sleepless night (6:1). What happened as a result?_____

_____

_____

D. Character Studies.

Make a list of traits of the following persons, as disclosed by these chapters:

Esther:

Mordecai:

Haman:

Xerxes:

III. COMMENTS.

The fate of the Jews throughout centuries of unbelief has been sad indeed. Wars, famines, broken homes, political upheaval, plagues and premature death were some of the judgments of the years of judges and kings. Then came the deprivations of the Assyrian and Babylonian captivities; coldness of heart in the four hundred years before Christ; and a worldwide dispersion to the present day for the rejection of the Messiah. The slaughter of millions of Jews by the Hitler regime reveals how much hatred the human race is capable of heaping upon a people.

The story of Esther concerns deliverance for the Jews during *exile* years. The book does not intend to extol the Jew, but to show that the fate of the nation—good or bad —is in the hands of a sovereign God. There have been tragic pogroms in the history of Israel, but there have also been miraculous deliverances, and the book of Esther records one such deliverance.

IV. A CONCLUDING EXERCISE.

What are your thoughts about the providence of God? How is this related to His attributes of love, holiness and immutability (unchangeableness)? Think back over the chapters of this lesson for some answers.

Deliverance of the Jews and Exaltation of a Jew

HOW THE JEWS SURVIVED EXECUTION DAY,

THE THIRTEENTH OF ADAR, IS THE STORY

OF THESE LAST CHAPTERS OF ESTHER.

In the last lesson we saw how Haman, key enemy of the Jews, was executed. The decree which Haman had persuaded the king to issue against the Jews, however, was irreversible, as were all the laws of the Medes and Persians (cf. Dan. 6:8).

I. ANALYSIS.

As you study the various parts of this passage, keep the brief outline of Chart X in mind:

ESTHER 8:1—10:3   **Chart X**

8:1	9:17	10:1 10:3
Deliverance of a People	Commemoration of the Deliverance	Exaltation of a Deliverer
Two Decrees	Two Letters	Two Men
Decree To Kill Decree To Defend	Feasting Fasting	Ahasuerus Mordecai

A. Two Decrees (8:1—9:16).

Observe what is said in 8:3-6 about the first decree. According to 8:7-10, who wrote the second decree?_____

_____

How does 8:2 fit into this situation?_____

_____

What was the content of the second decree (8:11-13)?

_____

What caused the Jews to rejoice (8:15-17) even though they knew the first decree was still in force?_____

_____

Read 9:1-16 and observe that the Jews' optimism was well grounded.
What do you see of the providence of God in these words: "In the day that the enemies of the Jews hoped to have power over them . . . it was turned to the contrary, that the Jews had rule over them that hated them" (9:1)?_____

_____

B. Two Letters (9:17-32).

Verses 17-19 describe what the Jews did when they survived execution day. Mordecai wanted to preserve this deliverance as a heritage for all generations to come, and so his first letter was sent to all the Jews to make this an annual feast holiday, to be called the Feast of Purim (9:20-28). The second letter (9:29-32) reminded the people of another aspect of the holiday, that of fasting.

What was the fasting intended to commemorate?_____

_____

_____

C. Two Men (10:1-3).

The book of Esther closes with a brief mention of what two men?* What attribute is ascribed to each?_____

_____

How many references to God's people, the Israelites, are made in the last verse of the book?_____

_____

How is 10:1-3 an appropriate conclusion to the book of Esther? _____

_____

CONCLUSION

Think back over the entire book of Esther. Recall that most of the book is about the desperate plight and providential deliverance of the Jews. Recall also that the problem originated over a religious issue: "Mordecai bowed not" (3:2). Because Mordecai refused to worship a man, he later received the blessing of God. Are you assured that God will always help those who honor Him?

Little did Mordecai realize, when he was serving in some minor capacity in the king's court, that one day he would be elevated to a position next to the king and, more important still, that he would be honored by his Jewish brethren as the Great Mordecai (10:3). His was the blessed privilege of seeking the welfare of his people, and speaking peace to all Israel (10:3). His own words to his adopted daughter Esther applied to him as well—"Who knoweth whether thou art come to the kingdom for such a time as this?" For without the royal favor of the Jews which he through Esther induced, there may have been no return of Jewish exiles to Jerusalem under Ezra and Nehemiah.

In these last lessons we have watched the movements of various characters in the book of Esther. However, who-

---

* No reference is made here to the death of Ahasuerus (Xerxes), which occurred in 464 B.C.

ever the character, the hand of God was recognized behind the scenes. The destinies of God's creatures are all part of a divine design, known fully to God alone. If chance determined those destinies, the world would have destroyed itself long ago.

> Yet the Hand that guides is hidden,
>   Moving secret and unseen,
> Managing, in life's great drama,
>   Every act and shifting scene.
> Nothing happens accidental;
>   All that men ascribe to chance
> Choice of God has first determined;
>   Nothing can escape His glance.
>
> A. T. PIERSON

Moody Press, a ministry of the Moody Bible Institute, is designed for education, evangelization and edification. If we may assist you in knowing more about Christ and the Christian life, please write us without obligation to: Moody Press, c/o MLM, Chicago, Illinois 60610.